Jo M. Cann

Politics and Policy-making in Northern Ireland

CONTEMPORARY POLITICAL STUDIES SERIES

Series Editor: John Benyon, *University of Leicester*

A series which provides authoritative and concise introductory accounts of key topics in contemporary political studies

Other titles in the series include:

Elections and Voting Behaviour in Britain
DAVID DENVER, *University of Lancaster*

Pressure Groups, Politics and Democracy in Britain
WYN GRANT, *University of Warwick*

UK Political Parties Since 1945
Edited by ANTHONY SELDON, *Institute of Contemporary British History*

CONTEMPORARY POLITICAL STUDIES

Politics and Policy-making in Northern Ireland

MICHAEL CONNOLLY

University of Ulster

Philip Allan

NEW YORK LONDON TORONTO SYDNEY TOKYO SINGAPORE

First published 1990 by
Philip Allan
66 Wood Lane End, Hemel Hempstead
Hertfordshire HP2 4RG
A division of
Simon & Schuster International Group

© Michael Connolly, 1990

Typeset in 10/12 pt Times
by Input Typesetting Ltd, London

Printed and bound in Great Britain by
Billing and Sons Limited, Worcester

British Library Cataloguing in Publication Data

Connolly, M. E. H. *1945–*
    Politics and policy making in Northern Ireland.
    (Contemporary political studies)
    1. Northern Ireland. Politics
    I. Title II. Series
    320.9416

    ISBN 0–86003–412–7
    ISBN 0–86003–712–6 pbk

1 2 3 4 5 94 93 92 91 90

For Sarah, Andrew and Una

Contents

Acknowledgements   xi

1 **Introduction: Northern Ireland – The Place and the**   **1**
  People
  Demographic and social background   4
  The importance of religion   7
  A relatively underdeveloped economy   9
  Conclusion: considerable political challenges   11

2 **Historical Background: From Stongbow to Partition**   **12**
  The most Gaelic part of Ireland   12
  The Ulster plantations   15
  William of Orange and the Battle of the Boyne   16
  Protestants as Nationalists   19
  After the Union   21
  The Great Famine and its Effects   22
  Agitation for Home Rule   23
  The partition of Ireland   25
  Conclusion: the stage is set   28

3   Creating the State: 1920–1939   **30**
The provisions of the 1920 Act   31
The Treaty of 1921   32
Westminster–Stormont relations   35
The financial position   36
The relationship with the rest of Ireland   37
Conflict within Northern Ireland   39
Catholic vulnerability   41
Law and order and special powers   42
The ailing economy   44
Conclusion: continuing enmity   44

4   Pulling the House Down?: 1939–1990   **45**
Developments in the 1950s   46
The rise of Terence O'Neill   47
1967 and beyond   49
Discrimination against Catholics   50
The debate about discrimination   52
The civil rights marches   54
Growing unionist dissent   56
The British army moves in   57
The downfall of Stormont   60
Direct Rule and Sunningdale   62
The 1974 strike and its political impact   64
Law and order   66
The Anglo-Irish Agreement   68
Conclusion: continuities and change   70

5   Government Institutions in Northern Ireland   **71**
Problems with the old system of local government   71
The Macrory Report   73
Local government finance   76
Current pressures on local government   77
Government by public agencies: education, health   79
and housing

Government by public agencies: policing and   82
employment
Northern Ireland government   87
The role of the Secretary of State   87
Governmental machinery   90
Central government under Direct Rule   92
Parliament and Northern Ireland   94
Conclusion: taking administration out of politics – 96
at a price

6 **Political Groupings in Northern Ireland**   **98**
The basic political divide   98
Two varieties of Unionism   101
The unionist political parties   102
Recent disagreements between the unionist parties 106
The loyalist paramilitaries   107
The Alliance Party   108
Two varieties of Nationalism   109
Conclusion: intra-communal party competition   114

7 **Policy-making in Northern Ireland**   **115**
Pressure for common standards   115
The Northern Ireland policy community   116
The policy community at work   121
Issues around the Northern Ireland problem   121
Finance and public expenditure issues   122
Other policy issues   125
The autonomy of the political process   126
The housing policy network   128
Policy implementation: the delivery of services   133
Conclusions: cohesion and a measure of autonomy   136

8 **Understanding the Northern Ireland Problem**   **137**
'Keeping the lid on'   138
The defeat of the Power-Sharing Executive   140
The importance of the strike   141
The Northern Ireland Assembly   142
The Anglo-Irish Agreement   144
Analysing the Northern Ireland problem   151
Conclusions: an intractable problem   160

References   164
Index

Acknowledgements

This book is designed for those taking A levels or a first-year course in British politics at a university or polytechnic. While it deals with the obvious, the book also hopes to inform students about some features of politics and political life in Northern Ireland that are neglected. In particular, there is a description of structures of government and some discussion about policy making.

In writing a book, one picks up enormous debts. A number of colleagues were helpful with ideas and information. I would wish to thank Andrew Erridge, Penny McKeown, Colin Knox, Sean Loughlin and Denise McAlister. Working with such colleagues is a pleasure and a challenge. My particular thanks go to Neil Collins, who read and commented on much of the book. John Benyon was a helpful and critical editor. The book is much better as a result of the efforts of John and Neil. I would also like to thank my copy-editor, Michael Ayton, and the various people at the publishers (especially Clare and Liz) who were extremely tolerant of academics and their foibles, as well as being extraordinarily helpful. Authors of books trespass severely on the time and good offices of children and spouse. My children certainly informed me about my offences in this regard on more than one occasion. My wife was more subtle in pointing out the costs of writing! In tribute, I respectfully dedicate this book to them.

1

Introduction: Northern Ireland – The Place and the People

During the last twenty years, to many people Northern Ireland has become synonymous with violence and bigotry. As Table 1.1 reveals, between 1969 and early 1989 nearly 2,750 people died in 'the troubles', including over 400 members of the British army, 177 soldiers of the Ulster Defence Regiment, 254 police officers and 1,848 civilians, including terrorists. In 1972 – the most violent year – 467 people were killed.

This image of Northern Ireland is the dominant one, and there can be no denying its potency. But it is not the whole of the story. In addition to the violence and fear, there is a great deal of stability. Health, education and many other public services are delivered, more or less adequately, to the people of Northern Ireland. Hotels and restaurants are increasingly busy. The retail trade is expanding, and the city centre in Belfast is usually full of shoppers, and has plans to expand shopping facilities. 'Retailers such as Marks and Spencers, Next and the Body Shop find that their Belfast stores make more money than most of their mainland outlets' (*The Sunday Times* 2 October 1988).

That is not to say that these activities are not affected by 'the troubles'. The aftermath of a bomb can seriously affect the number of shoppers for some time. But it is important to

Table 1.1 Number of deaths due to security situation 1969–89

	RUC	RUC'R'	Army	UDR	Civilian	Total
1969	1	–	–	–	12	13
1970	2	–	–	–	23	25
1971	11	–	43	5	115	174
1972	14	3	103	26	321	467
1973	10	3	58	8	171	250
1974	12	3	28	7	166	216
1975	7	4	14	6	216	247
1976	13	10	14	15	245	297
1977	8	6	15	14	69	112
1978	4	6	14	7	50	81
1979	9	5	38	10	51	113
1980	3	6	8	9	50	76
1981	13	8	10	13	57	101
1982	8	4	21	7	57	97
1983	9	9	5	10	44	77
1984	7	2	9	10	36	64
1985	14	9	2	4	25	54
1986	10	2	4	8	37	61
1987	9	7	3	8	66	93
1988	4	2	21	12	54	93
1989 to 30th April	3	–	4	1	21	29
TOTAL	171	89	414	180	1,886	2,740

Source: Royal Ulster Constabulary

emphasise that, despite the violence, a remarkable degree of what a citizen in Birmingham or Coventry would recognise as everyday life continues.

Part of the purpose of this first chapter is to introduce the subject matter and the objectives of the book. It is intended as an introductory text which will describe the main features of political life in Northern Ireland. The title of the book indicates the two main themes. The first focuses on the political conflict, a conflict that has claimed many lives and received enormous publicity.

The book also deals with an often neglected aspect of life in Northern Ireland. A great deal of the activities of public institutions are concerned with policies in areas such as education, health, housing and other public services. The book will aim to describe how decisions about these services are taken and how the wider political conflict affects them.

Charles Townshend has pointed out that 'Works of political science (about Northern Ireland) often have short historical introductions and long contemporary analyses' (Townshend 1983, p. ix). This book is no exception. The reasons are simple. Understanding current events without some knowledge of the past is impossible. Within Northern Ireland history is frequently used to justify current political attitudes and to generate much sloganising. The aim of Chapter 2 is to provide a brief historical introduction to the Northern Ireland problem, culminating in a description of the creation of Northern Ireland as a result of the 1920 Government of Ireland Act. Chapter 3 continues the story up to the beginning of the Second World War. Included in this is some discussion of those developments in the Republic of Ireland, and elsewhere, that have influenced politics and society in Northern Ireland. Chapter 4 describes events since 1945, paying especial attention to the period from the late 1960s when the current 'troubles' began.

Chapter 5 describes the main governmental institutions. Northern Ireland has a system of such institutions unique within the United Kingdom and it is important to see how they operate. Some attempt will be made to describe how political violence has influenced their development and operation.

Chapter 6 describes the main political groupings and their attitudes to some key issues. The following chapter aims to analyse how policies are made in Northern Ireland. In particular, it considers the degree to which policies in Northern Ireland are different from those operating elsewhere in the United Kingdom. The final chapter examines some of the solutions that have been offered to resolve the Northern Ireland problem. As these depend on how the problem is defined, there is some discussion about various conceptualisations of the Northern Ireland question and how it is analysed.

Demographic and social background

The second purpose of this initial chapter is to provide a description of some aspects of life in Northern Ireland. Political activity is embedded in a wider society and it is important to know something about this society. Hence this chapter provides a brief description of Northern Ireland's demography, society and economy.

As shown in Figure 1.1, Northern Ireland consists of six counties in the north-east corner of Ireland. These are Antrim, Armagh, Down, Fermanagh, Londonderry and Tyrone. It is described by a variety of names, a number of which betray political allegiances. For example Nationalists tend to dislike the term 'Ulster', pointing out that Ulster is one of the four traditional provinces of Ireland and is composed of nine counties: the six counties of Northern Ireland, together with Donegal, Cavan and Monaghan. Similarly, Unionists dislike the term 'the north of Ireland' as this seems to imply a unity in Ireland that they do not accept. They also point out that the most northerly county in Ireland is Donegal, which is in the Republic of Ireland.

In 1987 Northern Ireland had a population of 1.6 million people living in an area of approximately 14,120 sq. km., which is about 1,000 sq. km. less than Yorkshire and Humberside. (Figures are taken from *Regional Trends 1989* unless otherwise stated.) Compared with Great Britain (that is, England, Scotland and Wales), the population is younger. In 1985, 8.7 per cent of the population in Northern Ireland was aged under 5, compared with 6.5 per cent for the United Kingdom. Further, the birth-rate was significantly higher than the rest of the United Kingdom – 17.7 live births per 1,000 population compared with a UK average of 13.3 in 1987. Only 14.4 per cent of the Northern Ireland population was of pensionable age, compared with the UK average of 18 per cent.

The crude death rate is 9.7 deaths per 100,000 population, compared with a UK average of 11.3. This reflects the population structure. When one examines the age-adjusted mortality rates, a different picture emerges, as Table 1.2 illustrates.

In a number of key areas, the Northern Ireland health statistics give cause for concern. Northern Ireland has the highest

Figure 1.1 The four ancient provinces and the thirty-two counties of Ireland, the nine counties of Ulster and the six counties of Northern Ireland. (*Source*: M. McCullagh and L. O'Dowd, 'Northern Ireland: The search for a solution'. *Social Studies Review*, vol. 1, no. 4, March 1986.)

Table 1.2 Age-adjusted mortality rates, 1987 (rates per 100,000 population)

	Males	Females
England	1,120	1,096
Wales	1,179	1,123
Scotland	1,324	1,257
Northern Ireland	1,264	1,224

mortality rates for heart disease in the UK adjusted for age. The 'Ulster Fry' – one of Northern Ireland's more famous culinary delights, produced by frying egg, bacon, sausage, potato bread and various other items – has taken its toll. The perinatal mortality rates for 1985–7 were fairly high relative to the UK average, at 10.1 still births and deaths to infants under 1 week old per 1,000 live and still births.

Belfast is the major city, with a population in 1980 of 346,000. Boal (1987, p. 125) has described Belfast as

> basically a creation of nineteenth century industrialisation, growing from a population of some 50,000 in 1830 to 350,000 by 1900. Linen manufacture and shipbuilding were the central components of this industrialisation

This industrialisation also meant that the city's interests were oriented towards industrial Britain rather than agricultural Ireland. The political significance of this will be seen later on.

From about 1950 onwards the population of the city declined but that of the greater Belfast area increased (Boal 1987, p. 127). About half the population of Northern Ireland now lives in this area. Here the population density is approximately 359 persons per square kilometre, this figure increasing to approximately 2,900 persons per square kilometre. As one moves to the west and south the population density in general declines; for example, figures for the district council areas in the west show an average population density of some 53 persons per square kilometre in 1981 – exactly half of the Northern Ireland average (Greer and Jess 1987, p. 103). This illustrates a basic division in Northern Ireland between the Greater Belfast area and the rest – the former a substantial urban area and the latter predominantly rural.

Northern Ireland has an extremely varied range of landscape and scenery, 'with its diversity of compact mountains and extensive uplands, its lake-filled lowlands and broad valleys' (Buchanan 1987, p. 3). Within Northern Ireland the river Bann, which 'neatly bisects the Province on its long journey from the Mournes in South Down to the Atlantic coast of North Antrim' (Buchanan 1987, p. 3) is frequently viewed as the key geographical division. 'West of the Bann' is often used by those who live in the counties of Fermanagh, Tyrone and Londonderry, frequently as an expression of perceived isolation and neglect.

The importance of religion

Religion is treated more seriously in Northern Ireland than elsewhere in the United Kingdom. This is borne out in a number of ways. For example, only 8 per cent of men and 9 per cent of women who marry remarry: these percentages are the lowest in the United Kingdom. Some 86 per cent of marriages are solemnised by a religious ceremony, the highest percentage in the United Kingdom. Northern Ireland has the lowest number of illegitimate live births of any region in the United Kingdom (116 per 1,000 live births).

The Roman Catholic Church is the single largest denomination, with about 42 per cent of the population and 35 per cent of heads of households claiming allegiance (*PPRU Monitor*, No. 1/89). The number of Catholics in Northern Ireland has increased since 1921 by about 39 per cent (Compton 1987, p. 245). Between 1961 and 1981, the number of Roman Catholics grew at a rate ten times faster than that of the non-Catholics and, by 1986, Roman Catholics comprised about 40 per cent of the total population – compared with 34.9 per cent in 1961 (Compton 1987, p. 246). As Figure 1.2 reveals, by and large the percentage of Roman Catholics increases as one goes south and west.

Although the Roman Catholic Church is the largest single denomination, the numbers belonging to the various Protestant

Note: The figures show the percentage of the population in each district that is Catholic. The areas shaded are those districts in which Catholics represent over half the population.

Figure 1.2 Roman Catholics as a percentage of the population in the Republic of Ireland (95 per cent) and in the Northern Ireland District Council areas, in 1981. (*Source*: 1981 Census; M. McCullagh and L. O'Dowd, 'Northern Ireland: The search for a solution', *Social Studies Review*, vol. 1, no. 4, March 1986.)

churches combined mean that Protestants are in the majority. Politically this is the significant factor. The three main Protestant churches are the Church of Ireland, the Presbyterian Church and the Methodist Church, but there are also significant numbers of Baptists and members of various evangelical churches. Some 28 per cent of the population declare themselves as belonging to the Presbyterian Church, and some 20 per cent to the Church of Ireland; 4 per cent are Methodists and about 7 per cent belong to other Protestant churches (*PPRU Monitor*, No. 1/89).

A relatively underdeveloped economy

Northern Ireland has had a relatively underdeveloped economy for some time (see, for example, Harvey and Rea 1982; Rowthorn and Wayne 1988). As Birrell and Murie (1980, p. 191) put it:

> In relation to others parts of the United Kingdom, or indeed regions of the European Economic Community, Northern Ireland is an economically deprived region exhibiting all the features of a backward, peripheral economy with serious problems in its economic structure.

The structure of employment in Northern Ireland is markedly different to that of the rest of the United Kingdom. There is a much greater reliance on agriculture, construction and, particularly, the public sector. According to the Northern Ireland Economic Council (*Report No. 73*, 1989) public expenditure was equivalent to 65 per cent of the value of output in Northern Ireland in 1987.

In manufacturing, and indeed other sectors including agriculture, there is a preponderance of small companies. For example, Northern Ireland has a higher number of people employed in the manufacturing sector in firms with fewer than 100 employees than any other region of the United Kingdom, except for the south-east of England.

Unemployment in Northern Ireland is much higher than in other parts of the United Kingdom. In March 1989, unemployment was running at 15.7 per cent of the working population, having declined from the previous year's figure of 17 per cent. Over the same period, the unemployment rate for the UK as a whole declined from 9.1 to 6.9 per cent. In March 1989, unemployment in Northern Ireland was a full 5 per cent higher than in the North of England, which is the next highest unemployment figure (Northern Ireland Economic Council: *Report No. 75*, 1989). Further, if one becomes unemployed in Northern Ireland one is liable to remain out of work longer than elsewhere in the United Kingdom. Therefore, in Northern Ireland a person is 'more likely to become unemployed and less likely to cease to be unemployed than in any other region of the UK' (Northern Ireland Economic Council: *Report No. 75*, 1989, p. 22). This state of affairs is caused by Northern Ireland's high rate of population growth, lack of natural resources, long-term decline in key industries and remoteness from markets, as well as political violence.

Since 1945, employment in traditional industries of Northern Ireland, namely textiles, shipbuilding and agriculture, has declined steadily. In 1950, shipbuilding, textiles and clothing represented 66 per cent of manufacturing industry. By 1980, this figure had declined to 38 per cent (Harrison 1986, p. 54).

Up until the recession of the 1980s, this decline was more than made up for by the increase in services, particularly public sector services, and jobs in manufacturing attracted by the government's industrial development programme (Harrison 1986). Synthetic textiles and electrical and mechanical engineering industries were particularly important. Unfortunately, these new industries were affected, in some cases severely, by the recession of the early 1980s.

Given the high rate of unemployment, it is not surprising to find that Northern Ireland is poor compared with the rest of the United Kingdom. The gross earnings in Northern Ireland averaged £215 per week for full-time male employees in April 1988, lower than in any other region in the UK (though similar to the Welsh figure). GDP per head in Northern Ireland has consistently been less than 80 per cent of that in the UK over the past ten years (Northern Ireland Economic Council, *Report No. 75*, 1989, p. 8). In 1987, the GDP per head in Northern Ireland was only 94 per cent of that in the worst-off British region, Wales, and 65 per cent of that in the South East, the most prosperous region (Northern Ireland Economic Council, *Report No. 75*, 1989, p. 9).

A series of other statistics confirm Northern Ireland's economic and social disadvantage. For example, fewer households in Northern Ireland have a washing machine, or a freezer or a telephone compared with the rest of the United Kingdom (*PPRU Monitor*, No. 3/89). More people rely on social security in Northern Ireland than in Britain. The quality of housing is poorer than in other parts of the United Kingdom, though significant improvement has taken place during the 1980s. For example, 8.4 per cent of dwellings were unfit in 1987, compared with 4.6 per cent in 1986 in England.

Conclusion: considerable political challenges

What emerges from this picture is a relatively poor, relatively economically deprived region – a region which would present considerable challenges to a policymaker even without the political violence. The various social and economic problems are of course related to the violence, though the precise nature of this relationship is not easy to articulate. Each factor certainly makes the other more difficult to resolve.

2

Historical Background: From Strongbow to Partition

This chapter presents a brief historical background to Northern Ireland and its politics. This is important not only as a clue to an understanding of the forces and events that shape current political developments, but also because, in some senses, some of the language of current political debates in Northern Ireland comes from the past.

Exchange between the islands of Ireland and Britain had taken place from the earliest times. The distance between the east coast of Ireland and the west coast of Britain has never been such as to deter contact. 'Archaeological research shows clearly that Ireland had a close relationship with Britain and continental Europe throughout the prehistoric period; and the north-east of Ireland had a particularly close relationship with Scotland' (Doherty 1989, p. 13).

The most Gaelic part of Ireland

The modern political relationship between Ireland and Britain can be traced to the twelfth century, when a grieved chieftain in Ireland, Dermot, appealed to the Norman king, Henry II, to assist him in righting wrongs, both imagined and real, and 'changed the course of Irish history by doing so' (O'Corrain 1989, p. 52). The complicated twists and turns of twelfth-century politics, both religious and secular, need not detain us (but see, for example, Simms 1989). Suffice to say that Henry authorised his supporters to aid Dermot. Eventually he found assistance in Wales, where Richard FitzGilbert de Clare, better known as 'Strongbow', agreed to lead an armed force to Ireland to secure Dermot his position as King of Leinster. The conditions de Clare put upon his offer of assistance included marriage of Dermot's daughter and kingship of Leinster on Dermot's death. In 1169, Strongbow landed in Ireland, and won his military victory. In 1171, Henry came to Ireland to receive declarations of loyalty from Strongbow and a variety of Irish chiefs, though not from the high king of Ireland nor the northern kings.

If the Irish kings had hoped that they had made only token submissions they were mistaken. Henry appointed a viceroy, annexed a number of the important towns as crown demesnes and left garrisons in them. Further, the Norman barons, to whom Henry had granted lands, expanded their territories by driving out the Irish. By the middle of the thirteenth century, the Normans controlled most of Ireland, except north-west Ulster, while Connaught, that wild and rugged land in the west of Ireland, remained sparsely settled.

The Normans gave Ireland its first effective central government and cities. In those areas where their writ ran, Norman laws, customs and language replaced the Gaelic way of life. But the Norman conquest was incomplete. The Irish chiefs learned to resist and the Normans barons began to fight among themselves. Further, some of the Normans became 'more Irish than the Irish themselves' (Kee 1976, p. 10).

The area dominated by the English was known as 'the Pale'. It was centred on Dublin, expanding or contracting with English influence. The fourteenth and fifteenth centuries saw 'the Pale' dwindle, with a revival in Gaelic life and culture. But this period came to an end with Henry VIII, who determined to destroy the influence of the Irish chiefs and to establish his authority over the whole island. In 1534 his army, under Sir William Skeffington, landed and defeated an Irish army, led by Thomas, Lord Offaly, son of the ninth earl of Kildare and a member of one of the great Irish families.

Why King Henry's government engaged upon such a stern action is not clear, but 'it was partly motivated by the fact that the inexperienced Lord Offaly denounced King Henry as a heretic and declared himself champion of pope and emperor' (Canny 1989, p. 120). Henry could not afford to have an Irish parliament refuse to declare him head of the Church, nor to have his various marriages perceived as illegal in Ireland. When Elizabeth became Queen, an Irish parliament met briefly in 1560 and passed an Act of Supremacy, confirming Elizabeth as head of the Irish Church, and an Act of Uniformity, making the Book of Common Prayer compulsory. Religion had entered Anglo-Irish politics!

Ulster was to prove the most difficult part of Ireland to subdue. Before the seventeenth century, it was the most Gaelic part of Ireland, in the main successfully resisting English colonial ambitions. It was governed by a number of tribal chiefs, each of whom sought to pursue his own private interests and look after his own territory with a minimum of outside interference (Kee 1976, p. 10). Some measure of stability was afforded by the pre-eminence of certain of the tribes, particularly the O'Neills, the O'Donnells and the MacDonnells. There were, in addition, a number of customs and traditions that limited anarchy. For example, Foster records the existence of some local law-enforcement mechanisms, including the practice of 'fasting upon' an enemy to force him to arbitration, in other words going on hunger strike outside his door (Foster 1988, p. 11).

In the late sixteenth century, one of the most forceful attempts to end Elizabethan rule in Ireland was led by Hugh O'Neill, Earl of Tyrone, 'at once the last Gaelic hero and the first temporizing Irish politician' (Foster 1988, p. 4), and Hugh O'Donnell, Earl of Donegal. O'Neill had been given his title by Elizabeth, who hoped that he would remain loyal to her. His unreliability, as perceived in the Elizabethan Court, was the final straw and determined the need to resolve permanently the Ulster problem. Eventually, after considerable resistance, the armies of O'Neill and O'Donnell were defeated at the battle of Kinsale in 1601. In 1607, they fled to Spain, having abandoned all hope of restoring their position, an event known as the Flight of the Earls.

The Ulster plantations

In order to ensure that native resistance was permanently over-come, the strategy of 'planting' loyal settlers from England and Scotland had been used through the sixteenth century. In the main these 'plantations' had not been notable triumphs, largely because the settlers had tended to adopt the customs and prac-tices of the locals. But the Ulster plantations that took place after 1607 were much more successful. This was partly because of their scale and the determination with which they were pursued.

The plantations entailed the building of 23 new towns, described as the most important scheme for the building of towns before the end of the Second World War, and some 170,000 settlers, most of whom were the strongly Presbyterian lowland Scots (Arthur 1984, p. 2, who quotes Heslinga in relation to the point about the scale of building). 'What made it [Ulster] unique in Irish plantations was the comprehensive attempt made to attract, not only British gentry, but colonists of all classes, and the fact that the colonists were Protestant and represented a culture alien to Ulster' (Darby 1983, p. 14). In 1600, some 2 per cent of the population of Ireland were Scots or English. By 1700, that figure had risen to 27 per cent (Foster 1988, p. 14).

Most of the land that was confiscated was then granted out again in lots of one to two thousand acres at easy rents, 'on condition that those who received it should bring in Protestant tenants to cultivate the soil and build defences . . . for the safety of the settlement' (Clarke 1984, p. 191). The City of London was listed as undertaker for Derry, together with the former county of Coleraine and part of Tyrone. Special obli-gations (including the rebuilding of the ruined city of Derry' and privileges (including renaming the city as Londonderry) were given.

The theory of the plantations was that they would result in 'urbanization and segregation'. 'No Irish tenants were to be

allowed on the lands taken over by the major "undertakers" '
(Foster 1988, p. 61). In practice, this was not achieved. It
proved impossible to secure the rigid removal of natives from
their old lands. Therefore, native Irish and Planter existed side
by side. This contiguity left the native Irish resentful at seeing
their lands in the hands of others, and the settlers, particularly
the Presbyterians of Ulster with their strong religious ideas,
insecure.

In 1641 the native Irish rebelled. The Catholic Irish, from
both northern and southern Ireland, came together in an
attempt to win their confiscated lands. This enterprise became
entangled in the English Civil War, in which they supported
Charles I's losing cause. During this period, many of both
religions were massacred, probably in equal numbers, but the
initial blows were struck by Catholics. The events of 1641 were
seen by many Protestants as confirming all their suspicions
about their Catholic neighbours. The notion that Catholics
were never to be trusted grew out of 1641, and the myths of
that period remain potent.

The 1641 uprising was eventually crushed by Cromwell's
forces. Cromwell arrived in Ireland on 15 August 1649 and
embarked on his short but savage campaign, during which
he inflicted terrible suffering on the Catholic population. The
garrison towns of Drogheda and Wexford were destroyed. In
Irish Catholic demonology no one has a higher place than
Cromwell.

In fact, many of the poor and the men-at-arms were treated
leniently. Many of the latter were allowed to emigrate and
some 30,000 did so. Revenge was reserved for anyone who
owned land. This was expropriated from those involved in
rebellion. Catholics who could prove that they had not fought
against the English received partial compensation by having
land granted to them in Connaught and Clare.

William of Orange and the Battle of the Boyne

The restoration of the monarchy in 1660 revived the hopes of
the Catholics that their lands would be restored. But it was not
until James II came to the throne in 1685 that it seemed that

these expectations would be realised. Catholics were appointed to key administrative positions, including Viceroy, and an Act was passed returning the land.

This was prevented from happening by a new Protestant deliverer in the person of William of Orange. In February 1689 William III and his wife Mary, daughter of James, accepted the crown of England as joint sovereigns. James's Scottish supporters were soon defeated, leaving Catholic Ireland as his only hope. There Tyrconnell, the Catholic-appointed Lord Lieutenant, tried to hold Ireland for him.

During this period the great siege of Derry took place in 1689, 'which was to become the epic of the Protestant Plantation and provide its enduring watchword "No surrender";' (Stewart 1986, p. 61). Thirteen apprentice boys locked the city gates against the troops of James, and the city was besieged from December 1688 until the arrival of British ships on 28 July 1689. The commander of the garrison in the city, Lieutenant-Colonel Lundy, had wanted to surrender, but the citizens had rejected him and he had to flee in disguise. Even today, being called a 'Lundy' is an insult no unionist politician can easily ignore.

William landed in Ireland in June 1690, defeating James at the Battle of the Boyne, which took place on the twelfth of July of that year. James fled to France, leaving Sir Patrick Sarsfield to lead resistance. William returned to England. In 1691 William's forces won the decisive Battle of Aughrim. Sarsfield negotiated the Treaty of Limerick, signed on 3 October 1691. It was agreed that as many soldiers as wished would be given liberty and transport to France. Sarsfield and some 14,000 left Ireland.

'No surrender', 'Apprentice Boys' and 'Lundy' are all terms that are current today and continue to influence thinking and action. The Twelfth of July is still celebrated in Northern Ireland with a great deal of intensity. This period is important not only because the outcomes affected the historical developments, but also because of the enduring myths which it has provided. Catholic resentment and Protestant fears were formed all those years ago, and these myths are recalled in present-day Northern Ireland, and have a significant impact on current political debate.

In addition to providing some of the language of current debates, the aftermath of the seventeenth century structured events in Ireland – and hence in Northern Ireland – for over two hundred years. As Kee puts it:

> The Boyne and the other disasters suffered by the Catholics of Ireland between 1689 and 1692 marked the beginning of a long period, fading slowly in intensity over the centuries but not yet in the North wholly ended, in which to be a Catholic in Ireland meant automatically to be the under-dog. To be Protestant meant, whatever one's status, and by no individual effort of one's own, to be automatically superior. (Kee 1976, p. 18)

The inferior position of the Catholic population was incorporated into what became known as the 'penal laws'. These included provisions designed to exclude Catholics from Parliament and other official positions, to limit their rights as landowners and to curb their religion.

This close identification of religion with politics is not one that is easy for the modern age to understand. It can be dismissed as an aberrant Irish disease. Two points are worth making at this stage. First, in the seventeenth, eighteenth and early part of the nineteenth centuries the world view of people was heavily influenced by religious thinking. This is as true of Britain as of elsewhere in the western world. The identification of Protestantism with Unionism was no mere accident. As Stephen Bruce states: 'British civil society of the eighteenth and early nineteenth centuries was deliberately and self-consciously anti-Catholic' (Bruce 1986, p. 13). Ulster Protestants owed allegiance to a nation ruled by a Protestant monarch.

Second, it must be remembered that Catholicism and Protestantism grew up in opposition to each other. Again, to quote Bruce,

> Protestantism and Roman Catholicism were not *any two* different religions. They stood in opposition to each other. The former began as a 'protest' against certain features of the latter and, after they separated, each developed those elements which most clearly distinguished it from the other. They were thus fundamentally irreconcilable. (Bruce 1986, p. 6)

Protestants as Nationalists

While the divide between the Catholic and Protestant was never transcended, there were times during the eighteenth century when some reconciliation seemed possible. Three factors contributed to these developments, namely economic interests, internal division within Protestantism and external political forces. In the end, they were not sufficient to bridge the gap, but the fact that they applied at all has assisted in myth-building, this time on the nationalist side.

During the eighteenth century, Protestants in Ireland grew increasingly unhappy at the restraints placed by the English Parliament on their ability to trade. Their solution was an Irish Parliament, independent of their English counterpart but loyal to the King. Henry Grattan, a Dublin Protestant and lawyer, led this movement. Thanks in part to the example of the American colonists and the Volunteers, a Protestant militia formed to defend the country against invasion, the government conceded at least in principle. In practice, though Ireland was to be governed by the King, Lords and Commons of Ireland, Westminster continued to exercise control through the use of patronage.

Apart from the Americans and their bid for freedom, this was also the period of the French Revolution. A number of Presbyterians, the most famous of whom was Wolfe Tone (Elliot 1989), were attracted to the ideas of the revolutionaries. In this Tone and his Irish colleagues were not alone. As Marienne Elliot (1982) has pointed out, many people from different countries felt that they belonged to a wider reform movement. Tone, with people from all religions but predominantly with Protestants, formed the United Irishmen. Their aim was to break the connection with England, 'the never failing source of our political evils' (Tone, quoted in Kenny 1986, p. 7).

The story of the last five years of the eighteenth century – a period that saw the rising of 1798, the landing of French soldiers after two attempts and the eventual demise of Grattan's Parliament and the Act of Union between Ireland and Britain – is significant in a number of respects. The period has been romanticised by Nationalists. First, the appeals of Tone and the other United Irishmen for unity among Irishmen of all religions were high-minded, if doomed to failure. Second, their appeal was for an independent Ireland and this contributed to the development of nationalist politics.

This romanticism failed to come to terms with the sectarianism in Ireland, particularly in Ulster. There were frequent violent disputes between the Catholic Defenders and the Protestant Peep o' Day Boys, secret societies concerned to defend, if necessary by violence, each community. There was a contrast between the middle-class members of the Society of United Irishmen (and the Catholic Committee, which was formed to secure Catholic rights) and the peasants who formed these secret and violent societies. There was, for example, in the early 1790s a measure of conflict between the Catholic Committee and the Defenders, with the former condemning the latter, and the Defenders raiding their homes and treating members of the Catholic Committee roughly. Kee (1976) argues, with some justification, that the crude sectarianism of the Defenders militated against the sophisticated appeals of the United Irishmen to unity.

Similar tensions existed on the Unionist side. In September 1795, after what has become known as the Battle of The Diamond, in which a large party of Defenders attacked a party of Peep o' Day Boys, the latter formed the Orange Order. It consisted largely of working-class Protestants, and their activities were viewed, at that time, with horror by upper- and middle-class Unionists and Protestants (Kee 1976, p. 71).

The authorities reacted to the agitation and the external danger to Britain (because of the war with France declared in 1793) by attempting to pacify the Catholics through the Catholic Relief Act, by creating an Irish militia and eventually through police and military action. The situation, nevertheless, did not improve. In 1798 the ill-co-ordinated United Irishmen uprising took place, which was put down with savage efficiency. In truth, the uprising was never likely to succeed. The organisation, in so far as there was an organisation, was riddled with informers. Their only brief success was in Wexford, when desperate men fought bravely and, to their surprise, won a number of victories. However, in the end they too were defeated.

The United Irishmen in Ulster had either returned to Unionism or abandoned the cause due to military action and resentment at the sectarianism of the Defenders. The small group left could not even co-ordinate their uprising when it occurred.

The last hope was the arrival of the French. At the prompting of a number of United Irishmen, including Tone, the French attempted a number of landings in Ireland. Their ships appeared in Bantry Bay in December 1796 but gales prevented them from landing. French troops actually landed in Killala in County Mayo in August 1798, a story which is well told in Thomas Flanagan's novel *The Year of the French*. But they were defeated, as was another French expedition off the coast of Donegal in October 1798. Among the prisoners was Tone, who was tried and found guilty of treason, but committed suicide.

After the events of the '98 Rebellion, the government determined to ensure that they had direct responsibility for Ireland and, by a variety of means, persuaded the Irish Parliament to agree. The outcome was that in 1801 the Union of the United Kingdom of Great Britain and Ireland came into existence.

After the Union

At first a substantial number of Catholics were in favour of the Union. As Beckett (1981, pp. 273–4) points out, the bishops, landlords and middle classes were generally in favour, while the Orange Order were opposed, as were the old Ascendancy. Further, the British Prime Minister, Pitt, had let it be known that he favoured Catholic Emancipation. In spite of this, Emancipation was not achieved immediately and Catholic alienation from the Union grew.

It was not until the Catholic Emancipation Act of 1829 that Catholics were, by and large, granted civil liberties. This was due largely to the efforts of Daniel O'Connell – 'the Liberator', as he is known in Irish history (O'Farrell 1981; MacDonagh 1988). O'Connell used a loophole in the law to force the issue of Catholic rights. Although Catholics could not become MPs, there was nothing to stop them being candidates for Parliament. This is precisely what O'Connell did, standing for election in 1828 for the Clare constituency. He won the election, and eventually, in 1829, Catholics won the right to sit in Parliament and hold most high offices.

The manner of O'Connell's victory was important. He had mobilised the mass of the Catholic people and clergy in favour of his efforts. His organisational skills were enormous and, after Emancipation was conceded, it seemed that he could have what he wanted. But his victory was gained because of factors such as a divided Cabinet and a certain degree of Protestant and British support.

When O'Connell attempted to repeat the tactics to secure the Repeal of the Union, he ran into considerable difficulties. An important element in his tactics was the use of monster meetings. The government banned one such meeting – in 1843 at Clontarf, the site of a legendary battle in which Brian Boru defeated the Vikings. O'Connell, who had always stated that he did not wish violence and would comply with the law, cancelled the meeting. He never had quite the same influence again and he died in 1847.

The Great Famine and its effects

In any case, between 1843 and 1847 other matters came tragically to the fore. These were the years of the Great Famine (Green 1984; Woodham-Smith 1962). At the beginning of the 1840s, Ireland had over eight million inhabitants, 80 per cent of whom lived on the land. The majority of them depended on the potato for sustenance. When the crop failed, first in 1845 and then in 1846, the implications for the people were catastrophic.

Politically, the reaction of the government assisted in fostering the impression among many Catholics that, to put it at its mildest, the Union was not in their best interests. Sir Robert Peel, then Prime Minister, had initially reacted with speed and concern. He set up a scientific commission to investigate the causes of the disease and initiated a series of relief measures. But he decided not to prohibit exports of food from the country. Instead he repealed the Corn Laws. This brought down his government, which was replaced by one even more sympathetic to the then-fashionable notions of *laissez faire* economics. The Irish saw food exported from the country while they starved. It is not surprising that from this time onwards, as Beckett declared, Irish nationalism took on a new bitterness (Beckett 1981, p. 349).

The scale of the disaster is seen in that by 1850 the population had declined by about half. Many died. Many more left Ireland in what were known as 'coffin ships', going to America (mostly), Canada and Australia, taking with them in many cases a deep hatred of Britain. The political repercussions of this are seen today in, for example, the interest taken by many Irish-Americans in political events in Northern Ireland. There has always been a tradition of support among some of them for radical nationalism involving violence. Indeed the Irish Republican Brotherhood (IRB), the forerunner of the Irish Republican Army (IRA), was formed simultaneously in Dublin and New York in 1858.

It should be said that Ulster did not experience the same problems, or at least not on the same scale. This was so for two basic reasons. First, the state of agriculture in the province was better than in the rest of the country. This was due in some measure to 'the Ulster custom', by which tenants were not penalised for land and property improvements.

Second, during the first half of the nineteenth century, Ulster saw the beginnings of a rapid industrialisation. Belfast was being transformed into a thriving industrial town, based on shipbuilding, linen and engineering. From the 1850s onwards, there were 'spectacular advances in the shipbuilding and engineering industries until by the early twentieth century 48 per cent of Irish industrial workers lived in Belfast. . . . In economic terms Belfast was an anomaly, a British industrial outpost in agrarian Ireland' (Laffan 1983, p. 3). This in its turn had political implications as it helped to bind the Protestant community more deeply to Britain (Moody 1987, p. 277).

Agitation for Home Rule

While Ulster was more firmly supportive of the Union, the rest of the country increasingly opposed it. This opposition found its major expression through the Irish Parliamentary Party, though, as noted above, there was a significant element – the IRB, more popularly known as the Fenians – in favour of violence. The IRB is interesting for a number of reasons, and not only for its American connections which provided money and support. It attracted working-class support in a way other revolutionary movements did not. Furthermore, the Fenian rising in 1867, which was in many ways no more than a gesture, caused considerable alarm in Britain, helped no doubt by the fact that bomb explosions and other acts of violence took place in British cities.

Fenian actions, it is alleged, helped to awaken Gladstone's interest in 'the vast importance of the Irish question' (quoted in Moody 1987, p. 280), though he had previously had some interest in Irish matters, particularly the role of the Church of Ireland. Gladstone certainly believed that the Fenians assisted in making reforms in Ireland easier to secure politically in Britain. For example the Irish Church Act, disestablishing the Church of Ireland, was passed in 1869. This united various strands of Irish opinion, including the Dissenters and Catholics, as well as Gladstone's own party.

The Irish Parliamentary Party, whose most famous leader, Charles Parnell, was a Protestant, emerged at this time. The Irish Party fought on two interrelated fronts; securing land reform and Home Rule. These were the battles that the men of violence were also fighting, with the result that a series of alliances between Parnell and various leaders of extra-parliamentary forces were formed. For example, during the Land War, the Land League in parts of the country was almost an alternative government, setting up courts in an attempt to ensure that landlords did not impose too great demands on tenants. The objectives of the Irish National Land League were to preserve the tenants from being rack-rented and unjustly evicted in the short term, and to make them owners of their farms in the long term (Lyons 1973, p. 167).

From the very beginning it organised popular demonstrations against evictions. This developed into the tactic of refusing to rent land from which a farmer had been evicted. If anyone did rent such land, they were to be ostracised. In Mayo, one Captain Boycott, an agent for Lord Erne, was a famous victim of this policy, giving to the English language the word 'boycott'.

During the war of independence and following the 1918 General Election, Sinn Fein looked to this model and attempted a similar exercise.

During this time, Protestant influence on the development of nationalist thinking was important in one key respect. The late 1800s and early 1900s saw a considerable growth in Irish literary culture, in which Protestants played a significant part (O'Connor 1984). The list of such individuals is long and includes Douglas Hyde and W. B. Yeats. They contributed to creating a sense of the worthwhileness of Irish culture, language and sports. The impact of this development on political affairs is important, helping to support the idea of an Irish nationalism separate from Britain.

In 1886, Gladstone formed his third administration. His Home Rule Bill of 1886 was defeated in the Commons. A second Bill in 1893 was defeated, this time in the Lords, which was dominated by his opponents, the Conservatives. During this time, the fears of Ulster's Protestants about the situation increased, and there was a rise in various forms of resistance. The Orange Order, which had experienced some decline, now grew in strength and importance. Protestant resistance was strengthened by the opposition of the Conservative Party to any idea of Home Rule. To Conservatives, such a policy appeared to lead to the destruction of the United Kingdom. Arguments advanced by Liberals that Home Rule was the best way of preserving the Union seemed to them sophistry.

Despite this opposition, when a Liberal government was again returned to office, a Home Rule Bill was proposed and, with the support of the Irish Nationalist MPs, successfully passed through the Commons in 1912. The Lords again opposed it, but this time, because of the 1911 Parliament Act, they were only able to hold up the Bill for two years. It became law in 1914 but was immediately suspended with the outbreak of the First World War.

The partition of Ireland

Ulster opposition to Home Rule had not diminished in any way over the years. The two notable figures associated with this opposition were James Craig and Edward Carson, one a great organiser, the other a superb orator. In 1913 the Ulster Volunteer Force (UVF) was established. By 1914, the UVF were armed with weapons supplied from Germany and smuggled in on the ship, the *Clyde Valley*. The result was that when the Home Rule Bill passed through the Westminster Parliament, a provisional government was in place to take control of Ulster on the day the Bill became law.

Not for the last time did those who professed loyalty to the Crown set out to offer armed resistance to an Act of Parliament. Buckland (1981, p. 8), in explaining this, makes the astute point that political thinking in Ulster had not developed beyond that of the covenanting days of the seventeenth century. Then, contractual theories of governing were acceptable to many Protestants. They implied the notion that citizens owed conditional allegiance to their government. If the government broke the contract then the citizens were perfectly correct to resist by whatever means necessary.

While there were many in both Ireland and Britain who wished to see Home Rule killed off completely, an alternative began to emerge. The agitation in the north of Ireland had forced attention on to the question of whether Ulster should be treated differently from the rest of Ireland. While this would mean abandoning Protestant Unionists in the rest of the country, there were attractions both for Ulster's Unionists and their Conservative leaders. Many people in Britain had a measure of sympathy with Ulster's special case. A solution based on accepting that Ulster was different and should be treated differently from the rest of Ireland would have the ring of reasonable men willing to compromise.

For Liberals it was an approach that had much to offer. It did not help a party that was aspiring to secure votes among nonconformists to be seen to be coercing the Presbyterians of Ulster in the name of Roman Catholics. The government too needed to convince the British electorate that it was reasonable and willing to compromise. In addition, there was some doubt as to whether a military solution could be forced upon the province. The Curragh incident in March 1914, when army officers based at the Curragh military camp in Kildare threatened to resign rather than move against the north, strengthened the Unionist hand.

A number of ideas were canvassed to see if the wishes of Ulster and the rest of Ireland could be accommodated. Eventually the concept of partitioning Ireland was advanced. The Irish Nationalists in Parliament accepted the proposal that Northern Ireland should be temporarily excluded from the jurisdiction of the Home Rule parliament, but Unionists wanted this made permanent.

As a result, by the start of World War I the Irish question had still not been resolved. The suspension of the Home Rule Act merely deferred the problem and the Unionists found themselves in coalition with the hated Liberals in order better to prosecute the war. Many Irishmen of all persuasions enlisted in the British army. Numerous members of the Ulster Volunteer Force (UVF) joined up and they faced horrendous casualties at the Battle of the Somme in 1916. That year also saw the Republican Rebellion at Easter in Dublin.

The 1916 'Easter Rising' was led by a schoolmaster, Patrick Pearse, and a leading trade unionist, James Connolly. The rhetoric of Pearse has influenced the development of Irish republicanism ever since (Edwards 1977). Pearse had a mystical concept of the necessity of Ireland being saved through the blood of its people. His religious symbolism – for example his talk of the blood sacrifice and the desire that the Rising take place at Easter – was a feature of his republicanism. Initially, Connolly explicitly rejected Pearse's romantic blood symbolism, though he too took up this language as he came to believe in the interconnection between socialism and nationalism (Townshend 1983, p. 283). Furthermore, the commitment of the leaders of the 1916 Rising to a Republic has also been influential in nationalist thinking.

At first, the uprising was treated with tremendous contempt by the vast majority of the Dublin population, many of whom had relatives in the British Army. However, when the British decided to shoot the leaders of the rebellion, popular sympathy turned in their favour. Again, this has helped to bolster Pearse's position, in that his sacrifice apparently secured success from failure. The attraction for many Republicans of violent rather than parliamentary means owes a great deal to Pearse's political ideology.

In the 1918 General Election called at the end of the war, Sinn Fein won a resounding victory in Ireland, securing 73 seats against the Unionist's 26 and the old Irish Parliamentary Party's 6. In fact, Sinn Fein, meaning 'Ourselves Alone', was not directly involved in the 1916 Uprising. They were a political party, which had emphasised moral rather than violent resistance to British rule. Interestingly, West Belfast, now regarded as one of the most Republican areas, in 1918 returned an old-style nationalist rather than a Sinn Fein candidate.

After the election, Sinn Fein constituted itself as Dail Eireann (the Irish Parliament) and pledged itself to the Irish Republic that had been declared in the 1916 Rising. A vicious guerrilla war broke out, lasting from 1919 to July 1921, led on the IRA's side by Michael Collins. On the British side, an auxiliary force – the 'Black-and-Tans' – was created but, whatever their military effectiveness, their involvement in a number of outrages did not assist British political standing in the world, particularly in America.

During this time the situation in Northern Ireland had not remained static. Lloyd George attempted to impose a solution, and Parliament passed the Government of Ireland Act 1920. This accepted the argument that the situation in the six counties that now constitute Northern Ireland was different from the rest of Ireland. The Act partitioned the island and offered Home Rule to both parts of Ireland. Reluctantly, the Unionists in the north accepted it, fearing something worse. As described in the next chapter, the rest of the country rejected what was on offer and the war continued until a truce was agreed in July 1921. Further negotiations, involving Lloyd George, Michael Collins and Arthur Griffith, resulted in the Anglo-Irish Treaty of 6 December 1921 which established the Irish Free State.

Conclusion: the stage is set

In 1920, the future shape of the Northern Ireland state was set. Its precise configuration is described in the next chapter along with the 1921 settlement with Irish nationalists. What is perhaps interesting to note at this stage is that the growth of Irish nationalism was not inhibited by the resolution of various specific economic and political grievances. In some senses it can be argued that the resolution of such grievances cleared the way for nationalism to emerge as the issue. The point is that issues of culture – of taken-for-granted ways of thinking about the world – have to be considered if we want to understand political affairs. Such a perspective is important in understanding more recent conflict in Northern Ireland.

3

Creating the State: 1920–1939

The Government of Ireland Act received the Royal Assent on 23 December 1920. Neither northern Unionists nor Nationalists had achieved their central objective. It was accepted by Unionists as the only way they could remain within the United Kingdom. They had not fought for a devolved Parliament, but rather to resist what they saw as domination in a hostile Catholic all-Ireland. Their leader, and Northern Ireland's first Prime Minister, Sir James Craig, summed up their attitude in a letter to Lloyd George in 1921: 'As a final settlement and supreme sacrifice in the interests of peace the Government of Ireland Act was accepted by Northern Ireland, although not asked for by her representatives' (quoted in Lyons 1973, p. 696).

Northern Nationalists were appalled by the settlement. Not merely had they seen their hopes of participation in an all-Ireland Parliament, dominated by Nationalists and Catholics, disappear. But worse, the Act had placed them under the domination of Unionists: the option that they most feared. In one of those curious paradoxes of Irish history, the Home Rulers had come, in Northern Ireland at least, bitterly to resent Home Rule for the six counties, while those who had resisted Home Rule had come to accept it in preference to what they suspected would be domination from Dublin.

The provisions of the 1920 Act

The 1920 Act established, in the defined area of the parliamentary counties of Antrim, Armagh, Down, Fermanagh, Londonderry and Tyrone and the parliamentary boroughs of Belfast and Londonderry, a form of regional government unique within the United Kingdom (Birrell and Murie 1980). The 1920 Government of Ireland Act provided that the Stormont Parliament could legislate for the good government and order of the territory, except in regard to 'excepted' and 'reserved' matters. The former included the Crown, defence, external trade and international relations, and the latter most forms of taxation, postal services and the Supreme Court of Northern Ireland.

The Act also made provision for a Council of Ireland, consisting of twenty representatives from each of the Belfast and Dublin Parliaments. The Council was to have responsibility for certain matters, for example, railways. It was anticipated that reserved matters would be transferred to the Council, as both parts of Ireland moved together. This institution expressed the hope of some British politicians that there could be a measure of reconciliation between both parts of Ireland in the immediate future – but this failed to materialise.

The government and Parliament of Northern Ireland were limited in other ways by the 1920 Act. For example, Section 5 of the Act prohibited laws interfering with religious equality, while Section 75 of the Act left ultimate sovereignty of Northern Ireland with the Westminster Parliament.

Even when all these restrictions are taken into account, considerable formal responsibilities remained with the Stormont government and Parliament. In theory they could determine service provision for, *inter alia*: education, health, personal social services, law and order, housing, planning and economic development. In practice, their scope for manoeuvre was limited by policy initiatives in the rest of the United Kingdom and financial considerations.

Two Houses of Parliament were established: a Senate and a Commons. The former had modest powers to amend legislation and consisted of twenty-six members. Two (the Lord Mayor of Belfast and the Mayor of Londonderry) were ex-officio members and the rest were elected by the Commons in direct proportion to the party strength in that House. The Commons consisted of fifty-two members, elected for up to five years by proportional representation.

In order to assist in the administration of the services, a number of government departments was created under the Ministers (Northern Ireland) Act 1921. The Westminster model, with government departments headed by a Minister each of whom was responsible to Parliament, was adopted at Stormont. The departments were staffed by a separate Northern Ireland Civil Service (NICS). Initially, many members of the NICS were recruited from the old Irish administration, though some British civil servants were involved. The administrative machinery is examined in further detail in Chapter 4.

One further important issue that crucially affected the devolved Parliament was finance and expenditure. The essence of the arrangements was that Westminster retained control of finance but expenditure was a matter for Stormont. Taxation was predominantly a reserved matter. Northern Ireland was to receive a proportion of the revenue raised from taxes, after Northern Ireland's share of the cost of imperial services (such as defence and foreign relations), was deducted. This was referred to as the 'imperial contribution'. The amount was determined by a Joint Exchequer Board, which consisted of members drawn equally from the Treasury and the devolved administration, with an independent chairman appointed by the Crown. As Harkness (1983, p. 6) points out:

> . . . as a result of these measures, four fifths of the Belfast
> government's revenue came from London. . . . In contrast, four
> fifths of the expenditure was left for decision in Belfast.

The Treaty of 1921

This, then, was the system of devolved government that came into existence with the formal opening of the Stormont Parliament on 7 June 1921. The General Election held on 24 May 1921 resulted in James Craig, leader of the Unionists, becoming the first Prime Minister of Northern Ireland.

However, events during the latter part of 1921 threatened

further dramatic changes. King George V, in his Address at the official opening of the Belfast Parliament on 22 June, appealed to 'all Irishmen' 'to pause, to stretch out the hand of forbearance and conciliation to forgive and forget and to join in making for the land which they love a new era of peace, contentment and goodwill'. The speech helped to create the right climate for talks between the Crown and republican forces in the south of Ireland.

As outlined in the previous chapter, after the 1918 election, in which Sinn Fein won the overwhelming number of seats, the MPs constituted themselves as Dail Eireann and pledged themselves to an Irish Republic. Eamon de Valera became President of the Dail. From 1919 to 1921, the Anglo-Irish war, or 'the troubles', as it is referred to, took place. Eventually, a truce was announced on 9 July, to come into effect on 11 July 1921.

Negotiations began between Lloyd George and Eamon de Valera, with Craig available in London for talks and consultations if necessary. De Valera returned home with an offer of 'dominion home rule' to discuss with his colleagues. The Dail rejected Lloyd George's offer, but the British Government continued to deal with the representatives of the Dail. Finally both sides agreed to meet in a conference to ascertain 'how the association of Ireland with the community of nations known as the British Empire may best be reconciled with Irish national aspirations'.

Out of these negotiations came what has become known in Irish history as 'the Treaty'. This created the Irish Free State, which gave dominion status to the twenty-six counties. In theory this involved all thirty-two counties in the country, but there was provision for the six counties to opt out. If that option was exercised, which it inevitably would be, then a Boundary Commission would be established to 'determine in accordance with the wishes of the inhabitants, so far as this might be compatible with economic and geographic conditions, the boundaries between Northern Ireland and the rest of Ireland'.

Unionists perceived that their interests were under threat from the Treaty. They had believed that they had been given a promise by Lloyd George that Unionist interests would be 'in no way sacrificed or compromised' through the negotiations with Michael Collins and his colleagues. At the least, Unionists recognised the Boundary Commission as a threat, with the possibility of Fermanagh and Tyrone (counties with Catholic majorities) becoming part of the southern government's territory. Their anxieties were further increased by Lloyd George, who attempted to persuade Craig to take the devolved Parliament into the Free State.

During this time, the British press, including those who had previously been sympathetic to the Unionists' cause, urged them to offer concessions. Some of the reaction to the Treaty reflected the Unionists' feeling that they were being used by the various groups in Britain for their own purposes and that they would be abandoned if it suited these interests. Carson, in a bitter speech to the House of Lords, claimed that he was only a puppet in a game the purpose of which was to get the Conservatives into power.

If Unionists felt threatened by the Treaty, considerable numbers of those who had fought the British felt betrayed, though 'in Ireland the general reaction was one of relief' (Laffan 1983, p. 87). The Dail Eireann voted by a narrow margin to accept the Treaty on 7 January 1922. But there was a group – the irreconcilables – for whom the Treaty was unacceptable. The irreconcilables found taking the Oath of Allegiance to the Crown objectionable. The result was the Irish Civil War, which lasted from June 1922 to April 1923 (Hopkinson 1988). This reduced the military threat to Northern Ireland. But the Boundary Commission still remained, though the longer the northern state existed the less changes were likely to be introduced.

In fact, the Boundary Commission had no impact on territory of either part of Ireland. The Commission had decided to propose a very limited change in the boundary of Northern Ireland. In November 1925 there was a leak of their findings, to the distress of the Dublin government. The Irish Prime Minister, Cosgrave, reacted by requesting a meeting with both Craig and the British Prime Minister, Stanley Baldwin. This meeting reached agreement, which *inter alia* confirmed the existence of the border as it stood and pledged friendly relations between the two parts of Ireland.

This, then, was the unpromising beginning of the Northern Irish state. There had been consistent violence in both parts of Ireland for a considerable period. The Catholic minority was deeply alienated. But, by 1925, the state had a semblance of stability. Its development since then has involved four inter-linked trends, namely the relationship of Westminster to Northern Ireland, its economic and financial poverty, its relations with the rest of Ireland and the continuing conflict within Northern Ireland.

Westminster–Stormont relations

The British Government generally felt that the devolved arrangements that had been set in place meant that it could adopt a 'hands-off' approach to Northern Ireland and its problems. This was typified by a proposal for the abolition of proportional representation for elections within Northern Ireland. For a variety of reasons, Craig, Prime Minister of Northern Ireland, wanted to abolish proportional representation (Buckland 1981, ch. 3 and Harkness 1983, ch. 3). Westminster, alerted about the implications for the minority by Michael Collins, leader of the Dublin government, delayed giving Royal Assent to the Bill. However, the Unionists argued that one could not give devolved powers and reject the advice and decisions of the devolved Parliament on a matter within their jurisdiction. At that stage they held the ace, knowing that the alternative was to rescind the devolved powers, something which Westminster viewed with horror. Not surprisingly, PR was abolished and replaced by the 'first-past-the-post' system.

This established the nature of the relationship between the two governments and the two parliaments for the next forty years. By and large, Westminster left Stormont to get on with its own affairs, though there was a measure of Treasury involvement that is considered below. The relationship between the two parliaments and governments was confirmed by the inability of members of the Westminster Parliament to ask questions about devolved matters. This was due to a decision of the Speaker at Westminster, who in 1923 declared:

With regard to those subjects which have been delegated to the Government of Northern Ireland, questions must be asked of Ministers in Northern Ireland and not in this House. (*House of Commons Debates*, vol. 163, cols. 1,624–5, 3 May 1923.)

This remained the position until the mid 1960s.

The financial position

There was one area where the hands-off approach was not adopted, namely the financial relationship between Northern Ireland and Westminster. The reason was that the financial settlement contained in the 1920 Act presupposed that Northern Ireland had the same level of economic prosperity as the rest of the United Kingdom and was, therefore, fiscally viable. It quickly became obvious that this was not the case.

The Northern Ireland economy was adversely affected by the depression through the 1920s. As a result, there were greater pressures on the Northern Ireland Exchequer than it could handle. For example, the yield of taxation per head was significantly lower in Northern Ireland than in the rest of the United Kingdom (Buckland 1979, p. 83). The revenue from reserved taxation to Northern Ireland was reduced by 29 per cent between 1922–3 and 1930–1 (Buckland 1979, p. 84). There was a need to move from the system described earlier, which can be described as a *finance-based system*, in which Northern Ireland could spend what it could generate in funds (after paying its share of national expenditure), to one that was *expenditure-based*, in which the decisions on what public expenditure Northern Ireland was entitled to were first made, with HM Treasury making up the difference.

Part of the difficulty that the Northern Ireland government experienced was that they felt obliged to follow in broad terms decisions of the UK government. Expenditure decisions were based on notions of parity, of what the citizens would have been entitled to had they lived in Hampshire or Scotland. On certain items of expenditure, such as social security, the concept is easily understood. But ideas of parity on health or education are more difficult to define.

There was a range of regional and local considerations that complicated the issue further. The high costs of law and order added extra burdens. In addition, Buckland draws attention to the importance of local political pressures in increasing the burden on public expenditure. When these revenue and expenditure considerations are placed alongside the financial orthodoxy of the Finance Minister, Pollock, who, it is said, regarded a fiscal deficit as 'betokening not only political and financial but also moral bankruptcy' (Buckland 1979, p. 86), the fiscal difficulties of Northern Ireland can be easily seen. The solution was to seek aid from the Westminster government. Initially, this assistance was *ad hoc*, but gradually it became accepted that Northern Ireland had a case for something more.

The relationship with the rest of Ireland

Another consideration that influenced developments in Northern Ireland between 1920 and the 1960s was the relationship between its leaders – and its people – and those in the rest of Ireland (Kennedy 1988). While there had been some contact between Collins and Craig, there was, from the beginning, a fundamental disagreement of purposes between leaders from both sides. Northern leaders viewed with suspicion the attitudes and aspirations of the Southern Irish people. Northerners tended to view the Free State as dominated by the Catholic Church and interested only in taking over Northern Ireland.

It has to be said that this was not without foundation. In 1937, the Irish Free State's territorial claim to Northern Ireland and provisions on the family, education and property reflecting a Roman Catholic ethos were enshrined in a Constitution devised by the Taoiseach (Prime Minister) Eamon de Valera (Bowman 1982, ch. 5 and Whyte 1980). As Northern Protestants saw it, the 'malign' influence of the Catholic Church was evident in other instances, of which the Mother and Child controversy in 1951 is perhaps the most famous. In this case the Minister of Health, Dr Noel Browne, resigned because of resistance to his reforms of aspects of the health services for mothers and children.

There is little doubt that the Catholic bishops were unhappy with Browne's Mother and Child scheme, and expressed their opposition at a crucial time. A variety of groups argued then, and subsequently, that the episode illustrated the power of the Catholic Church. Prominent among these were Unionists, who in one pamphlet declared that the episode made clear that 'in any matter where the Roman Catholic Church decides to intervene the Eire Government must accept the church's policy and decision irrespective of all other considerations' (quoted in Whyte 1980, p. 232). Attributing Browne's fall solely to the influence of the Catholic Church leaves out of the story other significant factors, but the Mother and Child controversy certainly did nothing to break Unionists' perceptions of Southern Ireland (Whyte 1980, ch. 5).

There were a number of other elements in the 1937 Constitution which caused offence to Unionists. For example, there was the claim to the entire 'national territory'. Article 3 accepted that *de facto* the laws of the state could only be exercised in the twenty-six counties 'pending the reintegration of the national territory'. Article 4 provided for a change in the name of the state from Irish Free State to Eire, the Gaelic name for Ireland. Further, the Irish language was declared the first official language.

In addition to the 1937 Constitution, there were a number of other events which Unionists interpreted as anti-British and anti-Protestant. These included the Anglo-Irish trade war (1932–8), the abolition of the Oath of Allegiance and the return (in 1938) of a number of ports that had been used by the British navy under the terms of the 1921 Treaty.

Relations between the two parts of the island were not improved by the neutrality of the Free State during World War II. There was a great deal of resentment in Britain over the attitude of de Valera, with Churchill in particular deeply upset. It has been suggested that an offer of a united Ireland was part of the inducement to de Valera to join the war on the Allies' side, but it probably was never a real possibility (Fisk 1983). Though the Free State did offer assistance in various ways, for example in helping to fight the fires caused by German bombing of Belfast and in providing many personnel for the Allies' armies, its official neutrality did not help to create a good relationship.

In September 1948 the Irish Prime Minister, Costello, on a visit to Canada announced that the Free State was to leave the Commonwealth and become a Republic. This came into effect on Easter Monday 1949. The decision, which owed much to internal politics, further alienated both Unionist and British opinion. In this case the latter was significant, as the new Labour Government contained a number of MPs who were sympathetic to the nationalist position. The Unionist government's response was to hold a General Election in 1949, from which they returned with their usual substantial majority. The British Labour Government responded to Dublin's decision by passing the Ireland Act 1949, which contained a guarantee that Northern Ireland's status within the United Kingdom was secure.

Conflict within Northern Ireland

Relationships between the two communities within Northern Ireland remained tense, sometimes breaking into violence. Arthur records that between 1920 and 1922 nearly 300 people were killed, mostly in Belfast, in what amounted to a civil war. A curfew existed in the city until 1924 (Arthur 1984, p. 26). Harkness (1983, p. 77) records a catalogue of violence during the 1930s:

> The 1930s witnessed a number of unsavoury events which left the minority increasingly battered. In 1931, serious anti-Catholic riots in Armagh, Lisburn, Portadown and Belfast followed the prevention by the IRA of an Orange meeting in Cavan; in June 1932 the northern travellers to and from the eucharistic congress in Dublin were assaulted, and the security forces were seen to provide scant protection; in 1933 sectarian murder returned with the shooting of a Catholic publican in York Street, Belfast, an area where tension and violence was to remain throughout 1934. In 1935, riots in Belfast in May, June and early July were the precursors of the most serious outburst of the decade, between 12–21 July, when nine people were killed, scores injured and hundreds driven from their homes, with accompanying damage to property on a wide scale.

From the beginning of Northern Ireland, Catholics had felt alienated from the state. Some of the reasons have already been touched upon, but the essence was that the 1920 Act had delivered them, as they saw it, into the hands of their enemies.

There is little doubt that Unionist leaders did not go out of their way to accommodate Catholics. But there were senior Unionists who were aware that generosity to their Catholic citizens was politically, as well as morally, correct. For example, Edward Carson, on his retirement as leader of the Ulster Unionist Council, had given his colleagues the following advice:

> From the outset let us see that the Catholic minority have nothing to fear from Protestant majority. Let us take care to win all that is best among those who have been opposed to us in the past. While maintaining intact our own religion let us give the same rights to the religion of our neighbours. (quoted in Stewart 1981, p. 120)

Craig declared in 1921 that 'the rights of the minority must be sacred to the majority', and preached 'broad views, tolerant ideas and a real desire for liberty of conscience'. But eleven years later, he was to state from an Orange platform, 'ours is a Protestant Government and I am an Orangeman', and, in 1934, he told the House of Commons in Belfast that he was an Orangeman first and a politician and an MP afterwards: 'all I boast is that we are a Protestant Parliament and a Protestant State'. (The quotations are taken from Kennedy 1988, p. 61.) Lord Brookeborough, later Prime Minister of Northern Ireland, in a speech in 1933 stated:

> A great number of Protestants . . . employed Roman Catholics. . . . He felt that he could speak freely on this subject as he had not a Roman Catholic about his own place. . . . He would point out that Roman Catholics were endeavouring to get in everywhere and were out with all their force and might to destroy the power and constitution of Ulster. There was a definite plot to overpower the vote of Unionists in the North. We would appeal to Loyalists, therefore, wherever possible, to employ Protestant lads and lassies (cheers). . . . Roman Catholics . . . had got too many appointments for men who were

really out to cut their throats if opportunity arose. (quoted in
Barton 1988, p. 78)

The quotation from Brookeborough helps us to understand
Protestant feelings towards Nationalists. In those bloody times,
Protestants felt under severe threat and many believed that all
Catholics were united in wishing to see the state overthrown,
violently if necessary. IRA violence was certainly not uncom-
mon and there had been a number of savage incidents against
Protestants during the period before and after 1920–1, many
of which are documented in Kennedy (1988).

Paranoia thrived. For example, Foster (1988, p. 530)
recounts the story of Sir Richard Dawson Bates, Minister of
Home Affairs in the Northern Ireland government, who
refused to use the telephone for any important business in
1934, having learned 'with a great deal of surprise, that a
Roman Catholic telephonist has been appointed to Stormont'.
Foster drily remarks that the telephonist did not last (presumably as a telephonist at Stormont).

Catholic vulnerability

To be a Catholic was synonymous with being a traitor (Foster
1988, p. 529). Consequently their position was vulnerable. For
example, over time the proportion of Catholics in the civil
service, especially in senior positions, declined as the Orange
Order began to take an interest in such affairs (Arthur 1984,
p. 24). To quote Buckland: 'the divisions of the early months
[of the creation of Northern Ireland] became even more entrenched and the new government and Parliament failed to win
or even make a sustained effort to seek general acceptance'
(Buckland 1981, p. 59).

The major attempt by a senior Unionist to move across the
political divide was Lord Londonderry's efforts at education
reform. Londonderry

had a happy vision of all denominations being educated together
and his 1923 Education Act aimed to create an efficient system
of non-sectarian schools under public control to replace the

old and divisive system of inadequate and clerically controlled schools which had grown up under the Union. (Buckland 1981, p. 56)

However, this vision did not materialise, coming to grief on the rocks of both Roman Catholic and Protestant Church interests (Akenson 1973).

During all this time there was an impressive solidarity among Unionists. Some fissures had appeared during the Stormont election of 1925 and, during the inter-war years there were some signs of a Labour Unionism, but on the whole Unionist ranks remained united. Senior Unionist politicians were concerned that this continued. For them, the only issue of any importance was the maintenance of the Union and opposition to unification with the Free State. Politics was solely about this central issue, and it was only in the early 1960s that was there a possibility that things might change.

Nationalist representatives initially had boycotted the Parliament, and local authorities dominated by Nationalists had looked to Dublin as the source of the legitimate government. This policy of absenteeism did not last beyond 1925, ended partly by the agreement between Cosgrave, Craig and Baldwin mentioned earlier. Further, the Roman Catholic bishops had seen their interests compromised in the debate about reform in education and had urged the representatives of the minority to take their seats in order to ensure that the voice of the Catholic community was heard. None the less, it remained true that Catholics felt that they did not belong in the northern state.

Law and order and special powers

One of the most important areas in which there was considerable Catholic suspicion of the State concerned law and order. Northern Ireland had two law and order problems, the IRA and sectarian violence. In 1920, the British Government had essentially two forces to deal with these problems. These were the Royal Irish Constabulary (RIC) and units of the British army. Because of the scale of violence in the whole of Ireland, these forces were inadequate.

When the Northern Ireland state was established, legislation was passed to replace the RIC with the Royal Ulster Constabulary (RUC). The RUC was more militarised and more centrally controlled than any other police force in the United Kingdom. The head of the service was termed the Inspector General and was answerable to the Minister of Home Affairs. One third of all RUC places were to be set aside for Catholics but much fewer joined – by 1969 only 11 per cent of the force were Catholics.

The British Government also created, in 1920, the Ulster Special Constabulary (USC). This was based upon the Ulster Volunteer Force (UVF), the justification for legalising it being that it would be more easily controlled and, in its turn, help to control the wilder elements within the Protestant society. The USC was divided into three classes. Class 'A' was a full-time force. Class 'B' was a part-time force willing to engage in active patrol within its members' own locality. Class 'C' was a reserve force, willing to serve in the case of emergency. In the early days of Northern Ireland, the USC were the main peace-keeping force (Buckland 1981, p. 42).

In addition to developing this structure for the security forces, Stormont enacted a series of wide-ranging powers designed to enable the government to deal with internal violence. These were embodied in the Special Powers Act 1922, and provided the government, *inter alia*, with the ability to detail people without trial – 'internment', as it became popularly known.

Although, during the 1920s, there was evidence of violence from both sides of the community, these powers were used exclusively against Catholics. The consequences of this were twofold. One was to engender suspicion against the security forces among Nationalists. The second was to convince that community that the state was unalterably opposed to them. In Northern Ireland security became a way of life. The Special Powers Act was renewed each year from 1922 to 1972, with the result that there was an underlying tension between the security forces and the Catholic community. This was in spite of the fact that, in many cases, relationships were outwardly normal.

The ailing economy

There is one final point worth noting about this period. During the inter-war years the economy of Northern Ireland was severely affected by the great depression. The stable industries of agriculture, linen and shipbuilding were in decline. By 1939, the average income per head in Northern Ireland was only 58.3 per cent of the United Kingdom average – £64.70 as against £111 (Buckland 1981, p. 75). The state of the economy did not help to ease political tensions, though there were occasions in which it seemed as if workers from both communities might come together (Devlin 1981). This did not happen, however, and the depression certainly exacerbated communal strife.

Conclusion: continuing enmity

These, then, were the principal elements in the creation and development of the Northern Ireland state. It was born in violence and, for a considerable amount of its early history, violence continued. Two communities who had a long history of enmity were thrown together, one feeling threatened because the majority on the island had designs on their territory and the other feeling threatened because they were under the power of the other. The post-war period offered a new stage on which this old but deadly game was to be played.

4

Pulling the House Down?: 1939–1990

The post-war period saw the stirring of reconciliation within Northern Ireland, only to see this process collapse into the violence of recent years.

During the Second World War little changed in the political life of Northern Ireland. It is worth drawing attention to the neutrality of the Irish Free State, to which reference was made in the previous chapter, and to the ascendancy of Sir Basil Brooke, who in 1952 had become Lord Brookeborough, to Prime Minister. The Free State's neutrality widened the gulf between the two parts of Ireland; Brooke took over from the older and more lethargic Andrews and injected considerable energy into the war effort.

Brooke, however, was a bitter opponent of the minority in the 1930s, and it was 'perhaps an ominous portent that he was now at the helm of the province' (Harkness 1983, p. 104). He was to remain as Prime Minister until 1963 and his personality and brand of Unionism dominated Northern Ireland's politics through the 1940s and 1950s. Terence O'Neill, his successor as Prime Minister, commented on Brooke: 'As I see it the tragedy of his premiership was that he did not use his tremendous charm and his deep Orange roots to try and persuade his devoted followers to accept some reforms' (O'Neill 1972, p. 31).

Developments in the 1950s

The post-war period saw the Unionist government becoming more active in an effort to improve the economy and to introduce, however reluctantly, a modern welfare state. For example, the Industries Development (Northern Ireland) Act 1945 offered more generous inducements to firms to set up in Northern Ireland than did comparable British legislation. These efforts continued during the 1950s and 1960s, when there was a plethora of proposals emanating from various reports designed to improve the state of the economy.

The creation of the Welfare State in the rest of the United Kingdom posed a dilemma for Unionists. Unionist MPs at Westminster had voted with the Conservative opposition against much of the legislation which formed the backbone of the Welfare State. Expressions of concern at 'creeping socialism' were heard from within Unionist ranks. Nevertheless, Stormont, after some initial heart-searching (Harkness 1983, p. 106–7), recognised that Northern Ireland had to march broadly in step with the rest of the United Kingdom and many of the essential elements of the Welfare State were enacted.

The Health Services Act of 1948 followed the British Act in establishing the National Health Service in Northern Ireland, while a Stormont Act in 1947 implemented the education reforms that had been enacted in the 1944 Butler Act in England and Wales. However, Birrell and Murie (1980) argue that on a range of specific policies, particularly after 1948, Stormont lagged behind Westminster, for example on planning.

The overall legislative development necessitated a significant change in the financial arrangements between the two governments. In 1946, the principle of parity was accepted. In 1949 the Stormont and British governments reached the Social Services Agreement, under which it was agreed that if the cost of national assistance, family allowances, pensions and the health services was more than 2.5 per cent of the total UK cost, then the British Exchequer would pay 80 per cent of the excess (Birrell and Murie 1980, p. 18). Arrangements to cover national insurance were made in an agreement in 1951.

Despite some initial hesitation, therefore, Northern Ireland's social and economic policies grew closer to those in the rest of the United Kingdom. It was nevertheless still the poorest and most divided part of the United Kingdom. The political divisions showed few signs of unfreezing. Unionist leaders failed to appreciate the need to expand the basis for Unionism. In particular they failed to seize the opportunities presented by the Welfare State to bring Catholics within the Unionist camp.

The ambiguities within the Nationalist community emerged in the mid 1950s. At the Westminster General Election of 1955, Sinn Fein outmanoeuvred constitutional Nationalists and stood in all twelve Northern Ireland constituencies, winning two seats. This was seen by many Unionists as a sign that Catholics were supportive of the Irish Republican Army (IRA), but in fact was more in the nature of a tribal/protest vote. The evidence that this was the case was seen in the response of the Catholic community to the violent campaign launched by the IRA in 1956. This was a failure, due in considerable measure to the lack of support among the minority population. Many Catholics were feeling the benefits of the Welfare State and questioning their political position. The Catholic Church vigorously condemned the violence, while *both* governments in Ireland introduced internment without trial.

In February 1962 the IRA formally abandoned its campaign, charging that 'foremost among the factors responsible for the ending of the campaign has been the attitude of the general public whose minds have been deliberately distracted from the supreme issue facing Irish people – the unity and freedom of Ireland' (quoted in Harkness 1983, p. 131). For those seeking hopeful signs that society in Northern Ireland was becoming less violent and conflictual, not only was the lack of support among Catholics something to be welcomed, so also was the refusal of Protestants to react violently, as had happened in the 1930s.

The rise of Terence O'Neill

In March 1963 Lord Brookeborough resigned and was replaced by Captain Terence O'Neill. The next five or six years saw a continual thawing in the political ice, with a number of conciliatory gestures between the two sides. O'Neill took the most adventurous of these steps when he met the Prime Minister of the Irish Republic, Sean Lemass, at Stormont in January 1965. This stirred some controversy among Unionists, partly because O'Neill had not consulted any of his Cabinet colleagues, and partly because it was a central tenet of Unionist politicians to which he had given support that such a meeting would not take place until the Irish Republic recognised the right of the northern state to exist. In fact, at the time it looked as if the gamble had succeeded as most Unionist politicians appeared convinced by O'Neill's reasons.

Catholics during this time were rethinking their attitudes. They had benefited from the Welfare State and a number decried the barren nature of politics. A prominent Catholic, G. B. Newe, argued at a conference in 1958 that Catholics had a duty 'to co-operate with the *de facto* authority' (quoted in Phoenix 1989, p. 207). Arthur (1984, p. 90) makes the interesting point that at this time Catholic self-confidence was growing, helped by events in the outside world, particularly the election of Pope John to the papacy and John Kennedy to the American Presidency.

The Welfare State, particularly educational provisions, meant that a growing Catholic middle class could see material benefits from the Union, even if they still felt that discrimination existed. For that reason many of them were growing critical of the old politics that consisted simply of cries to abolish the border (see for example Harkness 1983, pp. 143–4, White 1984, pp. 43–5). Their attention turned to reforming, as opposed to abolishing, the northern state.

One of the most important examples was the creation in January 1963 of the Campaign for Social Justice (CSJ). The focus of the CSJ was discrimination and their role was to document it. It was partly their pamphlets that led to the foundation of the Campaign for Democracy in Ulster, a pressure group of Labour backbench MPs. For the first time, Westminster MPs other than those from Northern Ireland were starting to take an interest in its affairs.

During this period, there were stirrings of an ecumenical dialogue between Catholics and Protestants. It was hoped that this would assist in reducing division in Northern Ireland. But many of these ecumenical meetings were disturbed by the Rev-

erend Ian Paisley and his followers. These incidents convinced
O'Neill of the dangers of moving too fast – that among Unionists there still remained those suspicious of any changes. This
was further graphically demonstrated by the murder of a Catholic in Malvern Street, Belfast in June 1966 and a number
of other violent incidents involving the reformed Protestant
paramilitaries of the Ulster Volunteer Force (UVF).

The upshot was that O'Neill's modernisation policy focused
largely on economic planning and development. There was
little attempt to make the radical political changes that Catholics deemed necessary. They felt that economic and political
discrimination still remained virtually untouched.

> Even towards the close of the O'Neill premiership in 1969 a
> survey of 22 public boards conducted by the Campaign for Social
> Justice (CSJ) demonstrated that the average level of Catholic
> membership on these boards had reached only 15 per cent.
> (Arthur 1984, p. 99)

On the other side of the community, loyalists feared O'Neill's
modernisation which, they felt, might affect their position
adversely. O'Neill's approach gave rise to loyalist anger and
Catholic disappointment.

1967 and beyond

The increase in Catholic confidence referred to earlier, the rise
of a Catholic middle class, the coming to power of a Labour
Government, the example of the Civil Rights movement in the
USA and the language of the O'Neill government all helped
to contribute to the developments in Nationalist politics that
occurred in the late 1960s. A surge of protest took place, not,
at least in the first instance, against the existence of the state,
but in favour of increased justice, and involving more than the
traditional anti-Unionists. However, the veneer of increased
civility that Northern Ireland politics had taken on during the
1950s and 1960s proved too thin and in the end old passions
and enmities took over.

Initially there was an attempt to reform the state by

eliminating the major Catholic grievances. These focused on law and order, particularly the Special Powers Act, and economic and political discrimination. The principal pressure group was the Northern Ireland Civil Rights Association (NICRA), which had six basic demands:

1. One man, one vote in local elections.
2. Removal of gerrymandered boundaries.
3. Laws against discrimination by local authorities and the provision of machinery to deal with other complaints.
4. Allocation of public housing on a points system.
5. The repeal of the Special Powers Act.
6. The disbandment of the 'B' Specials.

Discrimination against Catholics

The local government system was a particular focus of criticism (Darby 1976, pp. 71–9, Cameron Report 1969). Three basic criticisms were levelled, against:

1. The limited nature of the franchise.
2. The alleged gerrymandering of electoral boundaries.
3. The alleged discrimination in the provision of services by local authorities.

To qualify as an elector, it was necessary to be a British subject at least twenty-one years old, to have been born in Northern Ireland, or to have resided continuously in the United Kingdom for the whole of the seven years preceding the qualifying date and to qualify as a resident occupier or general occupier. A resident occupier was an owner or tenant of a dwelling-house who had lived there or elsewhere in Northern Ireland for the preceding three months. The occupier's husband or wife also received a vote. A general occupier was an owner or tenant of land or premises (not a dwelling-house) of an annual valuation of not less than £10. Limited companies were entitled to appoint a nominee for every £10 of valuation, up to a maximum of six votes.

The consequence of all this was that the electorate for local government elections was about 75 per cent of that for Westminster elections in 1969 (Wallace 1971, pp. 52–3), and in particular areas of Northern Ireland the difference was even greater – for example less than 50 per cent could vote in Derry (Darby 1976, p. 50).

The Nationalist argument was that as the Roman Catholic community was less well off than their Protestant counterparts, the franchise kept more of the former off the electoral roll. This was of particular importance in the west, where Unionists either held a slim majority or were in the minority.

The allegation was also made that electoral boundaries had been drawn up with Unionist advantage a prime consideration. Bustead (1972) provides a number of examples of this practice, the principal one being Londonderry, where a judicious arrangement of the three wards in the City meant that, in 1967, eight Nationalist councillors were returned (all from one ward) by 14,429 votes, while 8,781 votes secured twelve Unionist councillors from two wards.

The third criticism was the alleged discrimination in the provision of local government services. Two principal areas of concern were identified, namely housing and employment. With respect of housing, a number of interrelated charges were made. For example, insufficient houses were built by local authorities, discrimination occurred in the allocation of these houses and finally, as Bustead expresses it, 'the siting of local authority housing was often planned with a sharp eye to the nuances of local electoral geography' (Bustead 1972, p. 34). Some councils, for example Fermanagh, solved the problem by simply not building any houses at all, but those that did 'behaved very much like Dungannon Urban District Council'. 'The Council had built, it was claimed in 1965, "194 houses in the East ward . . . and it allocated every single one . . . to a Unionist, to a Protestant" ' (Buckland 1981, p. 101; he quotes Darby 1976, pp. 74–5). In relation to local government employment, it was argued that local authorities, again particularly in the western and poorer part of Northern Ireland, discriminated against Catholics in local government employment.

The debate about discrimination

The allegations about economic disadvantage did not apply only to the activities of local authorities. As pointed out in Chapter 1, the predominantly Catholic areas were relatively less prosperous. It was argued that the regional economic planning approaches adopted by Captain O'Neill did little to redress this disparity. Allegations were made that little had been done to encourage inward investment to the South and West. In addition, the Unionist government on occasions took decisions which Catholics believed were motivated by narrow political considerations and illustrated a lack of concern, for example the decision to site the New University of Ulster at Protestant Coleraine rather than Catholic Derry (Osbourne 1982).

Unionists replied to these charges with a number of arguments. First, they argued that the Catholic claims were greatly exaggerated (Rose 1971) using, for example, the reports of the Commissioner for Complaints in support. Christopher Hewitt (1982, p. 364) has recently asserted that 'Catholic grievances have been exaggerated considerably'. He argues, for example, that the relative extent of Catholic disenfranchisement in local government was overstated, and that there were a number of local government areas in which a Protestant majority was governed by a Catholic minority. Hewitt (1982, p. 369), for example, concludes that in two rural district councils (Ballycastle and Limavady) Protestant majorities were governed by nationalist councils.

Second, the view was put that the reasons for the comparative Catholic disadvantage was that Nationalists had opted out of the system. In other words, their employment position reflected the fact that they did not apply for many jobs, particularly in the public sector. The standard reply to this argument was that, since Catholics were not going to secure these jobs, there was little point in their applying.

Many of these arguments from both sides reflect prejudice and the desire to defend already determined positions. What was needed was a proper understanding of the labour market. For example, jobs were often handed out on the basis of family contacts, without there ever being a formal process of advertising and so forth. Consequently, the social structure was often replicated in people's occupations, some of which were 'Catholic' and some 'Protestant'. Rhetoric replaced analysis on this issue. It seemed that each community preferred to stick to its position and not to try to resolve the real problem of disparity in employment patterns.

Third, Unionists alleged that Nationalist councils were equally guilty of discrimination (Newry was cited in the Cameron Report). The difference between the two traditions was not one of morality; rather, it was that Unionists were in a position to impose their will more effectively.

Finally, there were a number of Unionists who argued that such discrimination as did take place was justified by the alleged disloyalty of the Roman Catholic population. This latter argument was perfectly logical given the nature of the society and the symbolic and real importance of place within that society.

> Boycott, passive resistance and armed assault had all been used in attempts by members of the minority to bring down the state. How, Unionists were inclined to wonder, could such people be given public positions of trust, or allowed to dominate crucial border councils? The very reason for the existence of Northern Ireland was to protect the Protestant British heritage and Unionists were not going to hazard their achievement by enabling Catholic Irish Nationalists to wield power! (Harkness 1983, p. 79)

Londonderry is an example of an area with a large Catholic majority and relatively high unemployment, where patronage was a significant factor in finding or maintaining a job or house. It is also a city of great symbolic significance to Unionists, and it would have been a deep wrench for them to give control of the city's government to 'rebels'. It was not surprising that the City was a focus for the arguments of both sides.

The extent of discrimination has been the subject of academic as well as political debate. That Catholics did less well in Northern Ireland than their Protestant neighbours is accepted. Whether this was due to discrimination or for other reasons, for example because Catholics refused to participate in public life, or had larger families, or missed out because of the existence of key social networks, from which they were excluded, or lived in peripheral areas within Northern Ireland, is matter for argument.

Three points can be made. First, it was clear that Unionists did not help themselves in the debate. The speeches of some prominent Unionist politicians referred to in earlier chapters were frequently quoted by their political opponents. Few Unionists rushed to repudiate the sentiments contained therein. Indeed, some repeated, and even embellished, their anti-Catholic remarks.

Second, there is little doubt that some of the wilder Catholic charges were absurd. During the mid to late 1960s, some Catholic apologists were fond of comparing the Catholic situation with that of black people in the southern states of America, or even South Africa. Such comparisons had little basis in reality. Their only value was rhetorical. But they perhaps illustrated that such discrimination as existed has to be seen in the context of the way in which both communities perceived each other, and the enduring nature of their quarrel.

Finally, perhaps the most balanced judgement is that contained in a paper by John Whyte (1983). Whyte argues that, while some of the more lurid tales suggesting that discrimination was all-pervasive are not true, there was discrimination against Catholics. His view is that this was prevalent in some areas – electoral practices, public employment, policing – rather than others – private employment, public housing, regional planning. More importantly, discrimination was more liable to be found as one went west and south of Belfast.

The civil rights marches

1968 saw the civil rights debate taking place on the streets of Northern Ireland and in the media world-wide. The necessity for those seeking change to obtain maximum publicity beyond Northern Ireland was crucial. As Stormont was controlled by Unionists, it was necessary to ensure that Westminster took a more active interest in the affairs of Northern Ireland. The Campaign for Social Justice attempted to do this by keeping MPs informed with various publications (see McAllister 1971). The Northern Ireland Civil Rights Association (NICRA) strategy was to use marches, modelled on those of the American Civil Rights movement.

Protest concerning housing played a central part in the political violence of the late 1960s. In June 1968, Austin Currie (then a Nationalist MP in the regional Parliament and later to be Minister of Housing, Local Government and Planning in the short-lived Power-Sharing Executive) took possession of a house in Caledon, County Tyrone, which he claimed had been allocated on sectarian grounds to a Miss Beattie, an unmarried Protestant, while several Catholics with large families remained unhoused. 'In a sense the Caledon affair was a microcosm of the strong pattern of political influence in the location and allocation of houses throughout Northern Ireland' (Singleton 1982b, p. 77). Currie's action helped to focus Westminster attention on these issues.

The first civil rights march took place in August 1968, sparked off by the allegations concerning housing allocation in Caledon. But the first civil rights march that paid off in terms of gaining world-wide publicity took place in Derry on 5 October 1968. Part of the route of the march was banned by the then Minister of Home Affairs at Stormont, William Craig. A counter-march had been organised by extreme Unionists. The fear of a clash between the two marches was the explanation given by Craig for banning the NICRA march. This was seen by the organisers of this march as capitulation to intimidation. They refused to accept the ban and the march went ahead. The Royal Ulster Constabulary attempted to enforce the ban and violence occurred. Eventually rioting spread throughout the city.

The march and its aftermath helped to 'project Northern Ireland into British politics for the first time in a generation' (*The Sunday Times* Insight Team, 1972, p. 58). On 4 November 1968, Captain O'Neill met with Harold Wilson, the British Prime Minister, and James Callaghan, Home Secretary. In a speech the next day in the House of Commons at Westminster, Wilson attempted to sustain O'Neill in his reforming efforts against some members of his own party. Thus fortified, on 22 November 1968 O'Neill announced a series of reforms.

This reform programme included a commitment that all housing authorities placed need in the forefront of their criteria when allocating houses, and that future allocations would be carried out on the basis of a readily understood and published scheme. The reform package also stated that the Government intended to complete a comprehensive reform and modernisation of the local government structure by the end of 1971; to reform the franchise, including abolishing the company vote; to insist on a points system for housing; and to appoint a Parliamentary Commissioner for Administration to investigate complaints against the regional government. Further, Londonderry Borough Council was to be abolished and replaced by a Development Commission.

Growing Unionist dissent

While Terence O'Neill (1972, p. 107) later described the reforms as 'a small, timid reform package', they represented a substantial change in the context of Northern Ireland. Indeed, they were too much for a number of his colleagues. However, the reforms, together with an appeal on television on 9 December by Prime Minister O'Neill and the sacking of a persistent critic of reform, William Craig, two days later, eventually brought a temporary halt to street demonstrations.

This respite was broken by a march from Belfast to Derry organised by a student group – the People's Democracy. This took place on 1–4 January 1969 and was the target of considerable violence. A vicious ambush of the marchers occurred at Burntollet on 4 January, and there was rioting on the nights of 3 and 4 January in Londonderry.

On 15 January 1969, the Prime Minister announced an inquiry, to be led by Lord Cameron, into 'the course of events leading to, and the immediate causes and nature of, the violence and civil disturbances in Northern Ireland on and since 5 October 1968'. This was the first of many attempts to use an outside body of 'experts' to make difficult decisions. As Elliot and Hickie (1971, p. 61) put it: 'It was thought that the commission would end by recommending one man, one vote, which O'Neill could say he felt obliged to legislate for, against the stated policy of the Unionist Party.'

Some Unionists were increasingly unhappy with the conciliatory approach adopted by O'Neill, and a number of Unionist MPs had opposed the November 1968 reforms. A senior minister, Brian Faulkner, later to be Prime Minister, resigned from the O'Neill government, giving as his explanation the announcement of the setting up of the Cameron inquiry. Faced with growing Unionist dissent, O'Neill decided to appeal to the people over the heads of his party.

O'Neill called a general election for 24 February 1969, and this was an election that was significant in a number of ways. It was to be the last election called for the old Stormont Parliament. It saw the entry of Ian Paisley into electoral politics and the demise of O'Neill. Both communities experienced a degree of turmoil, as pro-O'Neill Unionists, both members of the Unionist party and unofficial Unionists, fought anti-O'Neill Unionists, both members of the Unionist Party and Protestant Unionists. In his own constituency, O'Neill was opposed by Paisley and, although the Prime Minister won, it was a close result. O'Neill secured 7,745 votes to Paisley's 6,331, while Michael Farrell, a prominent member of the People's Democracy, obtained 2,310.

The election had made O'Neill's position worse. He resigned on 28 April 1969, assisted on his way by a number of bomb explosions, thought then to be the responsibility of the IRA, but in fact the work of Protestant extremists (Harkness 1983, p. 155). The extremists believed that these explosions would discredit O'Neill's security policy and help to bring him down. In the last week of April, 1969, bombs deprived most of Belfast of water and, as O'Neill himself put it, 'quite literally blew me out of office' (O'Neill 1972, p. 122).

On the Nationalist side, members of the Nationalist Party were opposed by civil rights activists of various kinds. A number of these won, the most prominent of them being John Hume.

The British army moves in

Matters steadily became more polarised during 1969, particularly through the traditional marching season in July and August. During this time, a number of marches are held, particularly by members of the Unionist community, commemorating various events. In August 1969, the Apprentice Boys held their annual parade in Londonderry in a city tense due to previous rioting. The Northern Ireland Government refused to ban the march and, almost inevitably, considerable violence occurred.

The Catholic community in the city called for marches and other protests to take place in other parts of Northern Ireland. The purpose of this was to take police away from Derry, but it spread the violence. On the day British troops entered Derry, and the RUC and Specials were withdrawn, serious rioting occurred in Belfast:

> Protestant extremists vented their anger and frustration (backed rather than restrained, it seemed at times, by the Specials), burning houses, shooting and stoning in the lower Falls and Ardoyne areas. Patrolling RUC armoured cars fired their machine guns indiscriminately, adding to a death toll for the night of six. (Harkness 1983, p. 159)

British army units entered Belfast on 15 August, and after the arrival of additional units on the sixteenth, peace was restored. In the eyes of the Catholic community the IRA had not made much of a contribution to defending them. Indeed, graffiti in the Catholic parts of Belfast declared that 'IRA' stood for 'I ran away'. The anger of the Catholic community in Belfast helped restore the fortunes of the militarists within the IRA. The movement split, with the more political elements staying with what became the Official IRA, while the others formed the Provisional IRA.

The second major development from the riots of August 1969 was the entry of the British army, and, with it, increased interest on the part of the British Government. The Home Secretary, James Callaghan, visited Northern Ireland in August of 1969 and again in October. After Callaghan's first visit a communiqué was issued by the Northern Ireland Government, reviewing progress on reforms to date and announcing further measures, including the creation of a Community Relations Board and machinery for the investigation of citizens' grievances against local authorities.

UK civil servants became more actively involved in Northern Ireland matters. Subsequent to the Downing Street Declaration, working parties of civil servants, drawn from both governments, were set up to examine three topics: discrimination in public employment; the allocation and building of houses; and community relations. In addition, two senior UK civil servants were sent over 'to keep an eye on matters for [the British Government]' (Oliver 1976, p. 99). Oliver illustrates the distrust the UK Government had of the Northern Ireland administration when he writes that

> these officers withdrew from direct contact with our departments, set up elaborate establishments elsewhere and gradually built up a system of contacts and operations outside but largely in parallel with the ordinary stream of government business. (Oliver 1976, p. 99)

On Callaghan's second visit, and following a report from this working party, a joint communiqué from the two governments announced that housing was regarded as being in crisis. It was decided ('reluctantly') that 'the local authorities are not geared – and cannot be geared – to handle such a task and that the best hope of success lies in the creation of a single-purpose efficient and streamlined central housing authority'. This authority was to take over responsibility for the building, management and allocation of all public housing from the local authorities, the Northern Ireland Housing Trust and the three Development Commissions. This removed the most controversial function from the local authorities. A Review Body on local government was also created by the Stormont government in December 1969, under the chairmanship of Patrick Macrory.

There were also efforts to reform the Northern Ireland security forces. A committee under the chairmanship of Lord Hunt, the explorer, was set up. It reported on 10 October, making a number of important recommendations which were accepted by the Government. The B-Specials were to be disbanded and replaced by the Ulster Defence Regiment (UDR), still locally recruited but formally one of the regiments of the British army. Catholics were encouraged to join, and a number did, though many left after the introduction of internment in 1972. In addition, a number of reforms were proposed for the RUC. It was to be disarmed and demilitarised, becoming like a typical English police force. Sir Arthur Young, head of the City of London Police, was appointed head of the RUC. Unfortunately, the increasing violence caused the reversal of some of these changes.

Such reforms, though introduced by the Unionist Government at Stormont, were not to the liking of many Unionists who were already irritated over what they saw as a 'softly, softly' approach to law and order. Many Catholic areas, especially in Belfast, had erected barricades which prevented the police from entering them. The army was negotiating to have these barriers removed, but this was seen as pandering to Republican extremists. The publication of the Hunt Report, on a Friday night, was the final straw. Over that weekend, serious rioting took place involving loyalists. The police attempted to prevent loyalists from the Shankill Road in Belfast 'march[ing] to burn the Catholics out of nearby flats. And as they came down the street, they were halted by a cordon of exactly the police they were marching to defend' (Sir Arthur Young, quoted in Harkness 1983, p. 162). During this riot, the first police officer to die in the current troubles was killed.

The downfall of Stormont

Violence continued to increase. By late 1970, the two IRAs had emerged. The Official IRA was based on the old IRA while the Provisional IRA (PIRA) grew out of the anger of those in the Catholic ghettos at the inability of the old IRA to defend them. PIRA, supported by a number of Republicans from the Republic of Ireland and, increasingly, the United States, gradually became the more significant of the two. Relations between both paramilitary groups have not always been easy and on occasions murderous violence has broken out between them.

Through 1970 and 1971, both paramilitary groups began to wage open warfare, and bombings of city centres and shootings at security forces became more common. In July 1971 in Derry two youths were shot dead during riots. The Social Democratic and Labour Party (SDLP) demanded a full inquiry and decided to withdraw from Stormont until this took place. The IRA campaign increased in ferocity (Harkness 1983, p. 168) and with it grew the call for internment. On 9 August 1971 the Stormont Government, with the support of the British Government, introduced internment. This measure, which had been successfully employed in the past, proved to be a mistake on this occasion. Rather than diminishing the violence, there was a dramatic increase, with 23 people killed in the two days following its introduction and 144 by the end of 1971.

Many of those who were picked up in the initial swoop of the security forces were simply the wrong people. Nor was the situation assisted by stories of ill-treatment. The sense of Catholic grievance was increased as internment was employed only against suspected republican paramilitaries and not against unionist agitators. Many Nationalists opted out of various positions within the state. Internment had managed to unite the Catholic community against both the Unionist and the British governments.

A series of particularly bloody incidents, for example the shooting of thirteen people by British soldiers in Derry in January 1972 and the bombing of a Belfast city restaurant in March 1972, 'brought to a head the rift between Belfast and Westminster' (Buckland 1981, p. 157). This focused upon the issues of security and the role of political activity. The Belfast view was that the problem was essentially a security problem and that attempting to engage in discussions with the Government of the Republic of Ireland or anyone else was futile.

In London, however, that view was being increasingly questioned. The Conservative Government, under Mr Heath, suggested to the devolved Northern Ireland government that control of security should be wholly transferred to the London government. This was unacceptable to the Unionist Government, which resigned. One suspects that the British government knew this was a real possibility and probably welcomed its resignation. There is evidence that the policy option of removing Stormont and introducing Direct Rule had been considered as far back as 1969 (Bew *et al.*, 1979, p. 184 and Ditch 1977, p. 331).

Whatever the truth of this, Stormont was prorogued on 24 March 1972, and Westminster took direct responsibility for governing the territory, through the Secretary of State for Northern Ireland and his ministerial colleagues. The era of Direct Rule had begun (see Figure 4.1).

Direct Rule and Sunningdale

From the beginning, Direct Rule was intended to be a temporary expedient which 'was supposed to create the conditions for a new type of political accommodation' (Bew and Patterson 1985, p. 46). The British government's belief was that solving the problem required the co-operation of both communities. Hence its policy focused on securing a devolved government which had cross-community support (see for example the White Paper, *Northern Ireland's Constitutional Proposals*, March 1973).

The new Secretary of State, William Whitelaw, set about the enormous task of achieving this. The vast majority of the Protestant population were deeply resentful of losing 'their' Parliament, while Direct Rule would not satisfy the Provisional IRA. Indeed the only voices in Northern Ireland welcoming Direct Rule were the Social and Democratic Labour Party (SDLP) and the small moderate Alliance Party.

The British Government held elections in June 1973 for an Assembly which represented the first step in the implementation of its policy spelt out in the White Paper *Northern Ireland's Constitutional Proposals*. On the Nationalist side, the SDLP, which was in favour of the policy, won overwhelming support. However – significantly for future developments – Unionist parties opposed to the British Government's proposals won more support than those Unionists in favour (Bew and Patterson 1985, p. 56–7). Despite this set-back, and after much negotiation and pressure, particularly on a number of Unionist politicians, a devolved administration was formed, with politicians from a range of parties across the political divide becoming members of the Government. This was known as the 'Power-Sharing Executive'. Importantly, however, the two

'Stormont' Parliament*		Direct Rule from Westminster					
Unionist rule *1922 – 68*	Some reforms *1968 – 72*	Sunningdale *1973 – 74*	Convention *1975*	Anglo – Irish dialogue *1980*	Rolling devolution *1982*	New Ireland forum *1984*	Anglo – Irish treaty *1985 – present*
Majority rule	Majority rule	Power-sharing executive	Elected consultative Assembly	Inter-governmental discussions aimed at bypassing the deadlock	Elected Assembly	Constitutional Nationalist Assembly including SDLP and political parties in the Republic of Ireland	Established a consultative Inter-governmental Conference with Secretariat in Belfast to deal with on a regular basis with:
One-party government	One-party government	Council of Ireland	Convention Report favoured majority rule with committee role for Constitutional Nationalists	Review of the totality of relations within these islands	Power to be gradually devolved in proportion to degree of cross-party cooperation	Report favoured Unitary State Option	– political, legal and security matters – promotion of cross-border cooperation
	Administrative reforms Local government reforms Replacement of 'B' Specials by the Ulster Defence Regiment	Initiative defeated by Loyalist General Strike, May 1974	Report shelved by British government	Joint studies on possible new institutional structures, citizenship rights, security matters, economic cooperation and measures to encourage mutual understanding	Nationalist and Republican boycott	Outlined Federal State and Joint Authority Options	Joint declaration by both governments that any change in NI status will require majority consent
						All options rejected by British government	Boycotted by Unionists and rejected by Sinn Fein
1921 – 68	1968 – 72	1973 – 74	1975	1980	1982	1984	1985 – present

*The 'Stormont' parliament was suspended on 24 March 1972, and the Westminster government assumed direct responsibility for Northern Ireland.

Figure 4.1 Some of the political attempts to solve the Northern Ireland problem. (*Source*: M. McCullagh and L. O'Dowd, 'Northern Ireland: The search for a solution', *Social Studies Review*, vol. 4, no. 1, March 1986.)

major Unionist parties – the Democratic Unionist Party (DUP) and the Official Unionist Party (OUP) – refused to participate.

There was one additional element to the power-sharing arrangement, namely the creation of an Irish dimension through the formation of a Council of Ireland. Agreement on this was reached at Sunningdale. Much ambiguity surrounded this Agreement, with the SDLP declaring that it was an important breakthrough for the nationalist position while unionist supporters of power-sharing and some members of the British Government claimed that it was fairly innocuous.

The importance of Sunningdale is that it united all those anti-power-sharing Unionists. In December 1973, the United Ulster Unionist Council (UUUC) was formed, involving all significant unionist opposition to Sunningdale.

In February 1974, the British Government called a General Election. A number of Unionist politicians viewed this as an opportunity to test the popularity of the Power-Sharing Executive. At the election, within Northern Ireland Unionists opposed to the power-sharing arrangements won a majority of the votes and eleven out of the twelve Northern Ireland seats. In the United Kingdom as a whole, the Conservative Government was defeated and replaced by a Labour Administration. This resulted in a new Secretary of State for Northern Ireland, Merlyn Rees.

The 1974 strike and its political impact

Unionist hostility to the power-sharing venture and the Irish dimension now had electoral legitimacy. Throughout the early 1970s, a number of Protestants had begun to create a paramilitary organisation, the Ulster Defence Association (UDA). This grew rapidly, partly as a response to IRA violence. The growth of this and of other loyalist paramilitary groups indicated that British government policy initiatives had to take careful account of unionist reaction. The force of this was fully demonstrated in the strike which brought down the Executive.

This was organised by the Ulster Workers' Council (UWC), supported by paramilitaries. The UWC had been formed in late 1973 and had concentrated on recruiting shop stewards and key workers, especially in the power industry (Buckland 1981). The UWC strike began on 14 May 1974 and lasted fourteen days. It ended, after the unionist members of the Executive resigned, with the collapse of the power-sharing arrangement.

Chapter 8 examines some aspects of the strike and the Executive in further detail. It is worth noting here that the strike virtually ruled out the central plank of British policy, that is, an agreed devolved arrangement, and ensured that future attempts would have to be, if at all possible, immune from unionist reaction. It persuaded certain Nationalists that an internally-agreed solution was unlikely and spurred them to devote more attention to ensuring that politicians from the Republic of Ireland became closely involved in the Northern Ireland problem.

In May 1975 the Wilson government attempted to resolve the Northern Ireland problem by allowing its politicians to come together and propose a solution. To this end, they called an election for a Constitutional Conference. The United Ulster Unionist Coalition, made up of right-wing members of the OUP, the DUP and William Craig's Vanguard Party, was the majority grouping, holding 47 out of the 78 seats. As the Conference proceeded, Craig articulated the idea of a 'voluntary coalition' with members of the minority community. The essential difference with the Power-Sharing Executive was that the coalition was voluntary rather than statutory. However, the idea was rejected by Dr Paisley, and Craig was eventually defeated by Paisley's deputy in East Belfast at the 1979 General Election, partly because he was now cast in the mould of a moderate. The Convention was ended when the recommendation of the majority for a return to the old Stormont (or something like it) was rejected by the British Government.

During this time the violence continued, though not at the level experienced during 1972–3. There were two cease-fires, both of which involved British politicians talking with the Provisional IRA. The second of these occurred after talks between a number of Protestant clergymen and PIRA members at Feakle in County Wicklow in the Republic of Ireland. A cease-fire was agreed. The terms included the release of internees and the creation of 'incident centres' to monitor the cease-fire. This initiative failed, as was probably inevitable. The collapse of the Power-Sharing Executive and the failure of these talks to end violence meant that a new approach to law and order was required.

Law and order

Law and order policy increasingly developed two broad thrusts: 'Ulsterisation' and 'criminalisation'. 'Ulsterisation' meant that the RUC increasingly came to be at the forefront of implementing security policy – 'the primacy of the police' was the term used. The army was to be seen as supporting the police. One consequence of this was the increase in police casualties and a reduction in those for the army, though there still were some incidents which involved considerable loss of life among British soldiers.

Linked to this was 'criminalisation', the view that the activities of the paramilitaries should be regarded as criminal rather than political. This was reflected in the prison policy adopted. When Lord Justice Diplock reported in 1972, his main recommendation was the replacement, for what were known as 'scheduled offences', of jury trial by a single judge sitting alone. However, those convicted of such offences, as well as those interned, were to be accorded 'political status'. This meant that they had certain privileges, for example being allowed to wear their own clothes. The propaganda advantage to paramilitaries was that they could claim that what they did had a certain legitimacy as it was political, something recognised even by the British government.

From 1974–5, this approach was changed. Internment was ended. A committee under the chairmanship of Lord Gardiner was set up in 1975 to review the workings of the emergency legislation: 'Government policy on security . . . has been heavily influenced by the Gardiner recommendations' (Walsh 1983, p. 12). The central thrust of this Report was to argue that what was happening in Northern Ireland was *criminal* activity. It followed that political status should be ended as quickly as possible. Thus it ceased to be available to those convicted of offences after March 1976. There were some attempts to sweeten the leaven for example by allowing for remission of up to 50 per cent of a sentence, the most generous remission available in any part of the United Kingdom.

The ending of political status was not acceptable to the paramilitaries, particularly PIRA. When the first member of the Provisionals was required to wear prison clothes, he refused. Punitive action was taken by the prison authorities. The campaign against the new regulations was progressively increased (Clarke 1987). Prisoners wrapped themselves in blankets. Then there was the 'dirty protest', and finally hunger strikes. These saw ten Republicans starve themselves to death in 1981.

The hunger strikes were politically significant in two major respects. First, they led to Sinn Fein using elections as part of their strategy, putting up candidates for local council, Westminster and other elections as they arose. This in turn had other political implications. For example it caused Unionists to come into conflict with the government over attempts to have Sinn Fein banned. In addition it persuaded the Government – and the Irish Government – that the SDLP had to be helped if the Republicans were not to become dominant in the nationalist community.

Secondly, the hunger strikes increased inter-communal bitterness. Many Protestants were appalled that so many Catholics were willing to support the hunger strikers in their demands. In particular, the election to Westminster in Fermanagh and South Tyrone of Bobby Sands, the first of the hunger strikers to die, distressed many Unionists. Harry West, who at that time was leader of the Official Unionists and had opposed Sands at the by-election, stated that it was 'uncomfortable to find yourself living among 30,000 people who support the gunmen' (quoted in Clarke 1987).

The willingness of Catholics to support Sands, and, by and large, the hunger strikers' demands, in many ways illustrates some of the ambivalent attitudes to violence taken by both communities. Attitudes to violence are often conditioned by those who perpetrate it. To many Catholics, the truth of the hunger strikers' statements about the political nature of the violence was self-evident. It seemed to follow, therefore, that the hunger strikers should be treated differently (better?) from other prisoners. This position was supported by the belief of many Catholics, especially those who lived in strongly

Republican areas, that the security forces did not always deal even-handedly with the two communities.

Of course, many Catholics felt that some of the strictures upon violence of the Protestant community were hypocritical, in that a number of Unionist politicians appeared unable to take the mote from their eye when it came to Protestant violence.

For many Protestants such attitudes were repugnant. The IRA had murdered their friends, often in a cold-blooded manner. The UDR and police officers, in the main, were drawn from the Protestant community. Given the size of Northern Ireland, it was inevitable that most Protestant people would know security personnel who had been killed. In these circumstances, the demands of the hunger strikers were insulting and unacceptable.

The Anglo-Irish Agreement

During the 1970s and 1980s successive British governments increasingly accepted that the government of the Republic of Ireland should have some role in the resolution of 'the troubles'. This arose out of a variety of considerations. If violence in Northern Ireland was to be stemmed, then the Irish government would have to commit substantial resources to, for example, reducing the supply of weapons and ensuring that Republican gunmen did not have a safe haven.

The Republic of Ireland is a member of the European Community and various channels of influence are available to bring pressure on the British government. In addition, the significant Irish influence in the United States provides Irish politicians with a further channel through which they can influence British policy on Northern Ireland. It is important to prevent weapons and money getting to the terrorists, from America. The Irish government, as well as prominent northern Nationalists, can help to influence Irish-Americans. Finally, the Irish government has a special relationship with Nationalists in Northern Ireland, and might be able to influence them. It is no accident that the Foreign Office has always been sensitive to the Irish case. They are aware of the international implications of the Northern Ireland problem.

In May 1980, the British Prime Minister Margaret Thatcher and the Taoiseach (Prime Minister of Ireland) Charles Haughey reached agreement on co-operation. The phrase 'the totality of relations', used after a further meeting in December 1980, emphasised the extent to which they were committed to examining a range of possibilities for bringing about improvements. A number of joint studies were set in motion. In November 1981 it was recommended that an 'Inter-governmental Council' of ministers to review Anglo-Irish policy towards Northern Ireland be set up. Anglo-Irish relationships did not progress smoothly, however. The hunger strikes and the Falklands war caused tension between the two governments. This eased when Garret Fitzgerald became Taoiseach in November 1983.

The position was complicated somewhat in that James Prior, Secretary of State for Northern Ireland, attempted to generate a solution based on a devolved arrangement. His concept was of 'rolling devolution', starting with an Assembly with powers of scrutiny over the government in Northern Ireland. The hope was that the Assembly would develop and that governmental responsibilities for Northern Ireland matters could be devolved on to it. The Assembly met for the first time in November 1982. This 'rolling devolution' plan failed because the SDLP increasingly turned away from an internal solution and therefore refused to take part in it. The Assembly was eventually dissolved on 23 June 1986.

Garret Fitzgerald and Margaret Thatcher met in November 1983, after which the Inter-governmental Council started work. Eventually the Anglo-Irish Agreement was signed at Hillsborough Castle on 15 November 1985. While Article 1 stated that there could be no change in the constitutional position of Northern Ireland without the consent of the majority of the people in Northern Ireland, the Agreement gave the government of the Republic a right to be consulted in the governing of Northern Ireland. To this the Unionists took great exception.

The signing of the Anglo-Irish Agreement introduced a new and much more significant dimension to politics in Northern Ireland. The Agreement is viewed by Unionists as establishing joint authority over Northern Ireland by the Republic of Ireland and the United Kingdom. The British Government has offered reassurances that Dublin has only a consultative rather than an executive role, but these have been rejected by Unionists. Not surprisingly, the Agreement has caused considerable anger within the unionist community and provided a new focus for protests.

Conclusion: continuities and change

This, then, brings the story up to 1990. There is still a great deal of internal conflict. Attitudes between Unionists and Nationalists have not significantly altered in the seventy years since the 1920 Act. Furthermore, there is still a considerable amount of suspicion between the Irish and British over Northern Ireland.

Some matters have changed, however. The Republic of Ireland is now a respected member of the international community. The Welfare State and economic growth has made life more acceptable for the people in Northern Ireland, while religion no longer has the same hold over people that it had in the 1920s and before. The conflict increasingly is an international one, but the institutions and people of Northern Ireland cannot be left out of the equation and certainly must be included in any solution.

Chapter 8 will examine reactions to the Anglo-Irish Agreement in more detail. Perhaps the main points to make here are that Unionist anger towards, though not their dislike of, the Agreement has abated and there are signs that there is some rethinking about the way forward going on in that community. Within the Nationalist community there is a degree of scepticism about the benefits of the Agreement. Both of these feelings have been used by Secretary of State Brooke to attempt to generate talks between the main party leaders. By Easter 1990 these have not as yet materialised. In the meantime, there is no sign that the PIRA or other paramilitaries will cease their campaigns of violence.

5

Government Institutions in Northern Ireland

This chapter describes the main features of the institutions of government in Northern Ireland. Chapter 3 outlined the powers given to Stormont under the 1920 Act, and it was noted that this form of regional government was unique within the United Kingdom.

Despite periods of at times intense violence, this structure remained in place until the late 1960s. Then, as Chapter 4 explained, between 1968 and 1972 a number of important reforms were introduced. These resulted in local government losing a great deal of its powers, the creation of a considerable number of public agencies and, eventually, the proroguing of Stormont on 24 March 1972, with Westminster taking direct responsibility for the government of Northern Ireland.

Problems with the old system of local government

The present local government system dates from 1973, when the Local Government (NI) Act (1972) abolished the local government system then in operation, a system which had remained largely unchanged since it had been set up under the Local Government (Ireland) Act of 1898. The 1972 Act provides for the constitution of district councils to administer the

71

twenty-six newly created local government districts and for the regulation of such councils, including certain of their functions.

The political criticisms that were directed at the old local government system were outlined in the previous chapter. In addition, a series of criticisms were made about its efficiency and effectiveness. Under the old system there were a total of seventy-two elected local authorities, which, given Northern Ireland's population and size, was excessive. Throughout the post-war period structural inadequacies became increasingly obvious – there were too many authorities, many of which were too small. For example, there were twenty-seven local authorities each with a population of less than 10,000. Fifteen of the twenty-four urban district councils had a population of less than 5,000. In addition, some councils, especially in the south and west, were almost too poor to fulfil their statutory obligations (Birrell and Murie 1980, p. 159).

The Stormont government and local authorities themselves attempted to deal with this situation in a piecemeal manner. This involved both changing the administrative arrangements for particular services and altering the structure of local government. A considerable number of public agencies were created, in some cases to augment the work of local authorities and in others to displace them completely. For example, the Northern Ireland Housing Trust was created in 1945 to augment local housing services, while the hospital services were transferred to a Northern Ireland Hospitals Authority. An example of a structural change in local government occurred in 1967 in Fermanagh when the Borough Council and three rural district councils amalgamated with the County Council to form a single all-purpose authority.

Despite these changes, there was still considerable criticism of the system. For example, the Matthew Report (1963) had stressed the importance of local government in providing the appropriate infrastructure for regional planning and economic development, and was critical of the ability of the local government structure to undertake this task.

The combination of political and technical criticisms led to a number of proposals for reforming the local government system. But little of note occurred until the violence of the late 1960s, when the decision to remove housing from local government was taken. A Review Body, under the chairman-ship of Patrick Macrory, was set up to

> advise on the most efficient distribution under the Parliament and Government of Northern Ireland – whether under local government or otherwise – of the functions [of local govern-ment].

The Macrory Report

The Review Body reported in June 1970 and made much use of the Wheatley Report on local goverment in Scotland, adopt-ing its broad classification of regional and district services. The case for health and personal social services as regional services had been made by a Green Paper in July 1969. In this the government discussed the possibility of creating an integrated

Table 5.1 PRINCIPAL DELIVERY AGENTS FOR LOCAL SERVICES

	Government departments	Centralised boards	Area boards	Local government
Health			✓	
Personal social services			✓	
Education			✓	
Housing		✓		
Town and country planning	✓			
Roads	✓			
Water and sewerage	✓			
Recreation				✓
Economic development		✓		
Fire services		✓		

Source: Adapted from Birrell and Murie 1980, p. 174

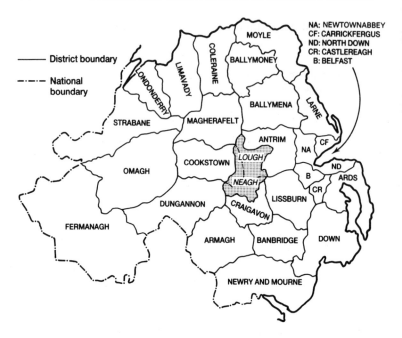

Figure 5.1 The twenty-six district councils in Northern Ireland.

health and personal social services system. Macrory judged a number of other services to be regional, and these became the responsibility of area boards (for example, education and library services), government departments (for example, the Department of the Environment in Northern Ireland [DOE NI] acquired direct responsibility for planning, roads, water and sewerage), or a centralised *ad hoc* board (for example, the fire service). Table 5.1 gives particulars.

What, then, were to be the structure and functions of local government? The Report argued for a reduction in the number of local authorities from seventy-two assorted local authorities to twenty-six district councils, based upon 'the main centres' (Macrory Report 1970, para. 114). Figure 5.1 shows the 26 local government districts. The number seems to have been based upon taking the then existing number of borough and urban districts (35) and removing those the Review Body considered were not 'main centres of district activity' (para. 114, p. 39).

Macrory indicated that these local authorities were to have four broad functions: *ceremonial, executive, representative* and *consultative.*

1. **Ceremonial functions** refer to the dignities and ceremonial traditionally attached to local government, such as allowing local authorities to become boroughs, with the chairman of the council being entitled to be called mayor.

2. **Executive functions** can be considered under three headings:
   (a) *regulatory services*, for example licensing of cinemas and dance-halls, and street-trading, building regulations, health inspection;
   (b) *provision of certain services*, including street cleaning, refuse collection and disposal, burial grounds and crematoria, public baths, recreation facilities and tourist amenities;
   (c) *other functions*, for example the ability to spend certain monies for the general welfare of the people within the area.

3. **Representative functions** mean, according to Macrory, that local councillors should be represented on relevant bodies, such as the area boards, so as to 'express views on the provision and operation of . . . public services in their area' (Macrory Report 1970, para. 123, p. 43).

4. **Consultative functions** mean that the district councils should be consulted on matters of 'general national interest' (Macrory Report 1970, para. 124, p. 43). In addition, councils should be consulted on matters which are the responsibility of central government but which affect their area, for example planning applications, housing and roads.

One of the interesting features of the Macrory Report, and indeed of many of the other official documents of the time on administrative reforms, was how little discussion was devoted to the political divisions in the society. It was as though the reform of local government was purely an administrative and technical problem. One may speculate that this was because those charged with producing the Report used this approach in order to avoid charges of political bias. It makes considerable sense to administrators and professionals to preserve a degree of aloofness from sectarian politics.

The electoral system was also reformed at this time. The Single Transferable Vote (STV) system of proportional representation was re-introduced under the Electoral Law (Northern Ireland) Order 1972, initially as an experiment. In 1977 the Northern Ireland (Local Election) Order provided for STV to be used for all future district council elections. The reform was introduced despite considerable unionist opposition.

Local government finance

It is also worth commenting briefly on the system of local government finance in Northern Ireland. As is traditional there is a distinction made between revenue and capital. Local authorities obtain monies for their revenue expenditure from grants, rates and fees (Connolly 1986). Most of the grant monies come from a General Grant which has two elements. One is a de-rating element the principal purpose of which is to compensate local authorities for loss of rate income due to the de-rating of certain property. The second element is a resources element which aims to support the poorer authorities. The grant makes up about 40 per cent of the total income for rate support services.

Grants are of crucial importance to local authorities when considering capital expenditure. Without them many projects could not take place and councils would normally not consider going forward with a major new venture without securing one. There are exceptions but they are rare. The major capital grants are provided for a specific purpose, with grants for leisure facilities particularly prominent.

While local government finance in the rest of the United Kingdom has been subject to much controversy and change, this has not been the case in Northern Ireland. The system has been stable. Unlike Scotland, Wales and England, thus far there has been no suggestion that a poll tax will be introduced into Northern Ireland. The reasons for this are not hard to find. Local authority expenditure is a relatively small part of total public expenditure in Northern Ireland and central government feels it has adequate control mechanisms. Capital expenditure is heavily dependent on central government.

In addition, the total rates bill that a ratepayer receives consists of two elements, a regional rate, which is levied by central government, and the district rate, determined by the local authority of the district within which the ratepayer lives. The former element is intended to reflect the fact that many services that are provided by local authorities in Britain are provided by central government in Northern Ireland. As these are the majority of services, it is not surprising that the greater part (about two-thirds) of the total rates bill is determined by central government. For all of these reasons there would be little to be gained from changing to a poll tax system.

Current pressures on local government

Despite the relative lack of powers of local government in the territory, it has not been a stranger to controversy. The election of considerable numbers of Sinn Fein councillors in the 1985 local government elections and the signing of the Anglo-Irish Agreement in November 1985 caused considerable disruption for many local authorities. Unionists wish to see Sinn Fein, the political wing of the Provisional IRA, banned, and to that end undertook during 1985 a series of protest actions, including continual adjournment of councils.

These protests were overtaken by the passionate unionist opposition to the Anglo-Irish agreement. Unionist councils intensified their protests, which brought them into confrontation with the courts (Sinclair 1986). Nevertheless, many Unionists were uneasy about this and subsequently the councils gradually returned to normal working (Connolly and Knox 1988).

More recently, the Government has produced a consultative paper on local government. This has three parts. The first was a reaction to the protests in the local authorities. It proposed that increased powers be given to chief executives and that local authorities should adopt a prescribed core of standing orders. This was thought necessary to avoid some of the activities, particularly those aimed against minority groups on councils, that some councils practised. The second section was concerned with tidying up the administration of the environmental health and building control services. The third part proposed the introduction of compulsory competitive tendering in local government. The introduction of this latter proposal would have serious implications for the already denuded local government system in Northern Ireland (Knox 1989).

In addition to the consultative paper, in October 1988 the Government issued a notice requiring the BBC and IBA to refrain from broadcasting direct statements by proscribed organisations. Further, on 24 November 1988 the Government published the Elected Authorities (Northern Ireland) Bill. This required those who aspire to election for local government to declare that they did not support the activities of any banned organisation, nor espouse or approve of any acts of violence. The declaration was to be signed at nomination stage, but did not apply during the campaign. Enforcement lay with individual councillors and/or ratepayers, who will have to take a civil action.

Unionists complained about both the provisions and enforcement of the measures. They wished to see Sinn Fein banned. Certainly, if that was the intention behind the Government's approach, the experiences during the 1989 local government elections suggested failure. Sinn Fein candidates signed any declaration that was required of them. Whether the range of government measures had any effect on their electoral prospects is more difficult to say, as the Social Democratic and Labour Party (SDLP) made some inroads against Sinn Fein.

Despite its lack of powers, the controversy associated with local government is easily understood. It is the only mechanism of elected democratic control over local services, the major channel through which local politicians influence regional services, the only forum where the impact of services can be considered and debated, and the only set of institutions in Northern Ireland through which political divisions can be formally aired. In some senses the very paucity of local government services means that local councillors seeking a role must find it in wider political issues.

Government by public agencies: education, health and housing

As a result of the 1972 local government reforms there was a considerable increase in the centralisation of decision-making in Northern Ireland. One aspect of this has been a recourse to the use of public agencies of various types. Northern Ireland has not been unique in attempting to manage public policy through endeavouring to depoliticise it, but this approach to policy management has perhaps gone further than elsewhere in the United Kindom.

To some extent, this attempt at depoliticisation reflects a widespread tendency to distrust politicians and a view that services are best left to professionals and administrators. But, in the main, it is an attempt to escape some of the baser features of sectarian politics. The result is that, as Table 5.1 indicates, a wide range of services in Northern Ireland is managed by public agencies. It is worth describing some of the main ones, particularly where they differ from those in other parts of the United Kingdom.

Area boards

Education and related services, as well as health and personal social services, are managed through area boards. There are five education and library boards and four health and social services boards. The boards comprise individuals drawn from local government, professional bodies, interested groups and other local people, all appointed by the relevant minister. With respect to the education and library services, 40 per cent of board members are local councillors – appointed by the minister following nomination by their respective councils – while for the health and personal social services the figure is 30 per cent.

Relationships between boards and their respective departments are on occasions fraught, but there can be little doubt that the department is the dominant partner. It has been argued that every education decision, great or small, is vetted by the Department of Education Northern Ireland (DENI) before it is made by the boards (Connolly 1983). The boards receive virtually all their money from their respective department, and they are accountable to the department for their expenditure. They have to operate within departmental policy guidelines. In addition, the health and personal social service boards are formally defined as agents of the Department of Health and Social Services, which also owns the various health care facilities.

The Northern Ireland Housing Executive (NIHE)

Despite improvements in recent years, Northern Ireland has the worst housing conditions in the United Kingdom. Housing has also been a major political issue with significant sectarian dimensions. The combination of these factors resulted in the removal of housing from the local authorities and the creation of the Northern Ireland Housing Executive (NIHE) as a comprehensive public housing agency, unique in the United Kingdom (Birrell and Murie 1980, Singleton 1982b). It came into being in October 1972 and by July 1973 it had taken over responsibility for public housing, as well as certain responsibilities in respect of the private sector.

The NIHE is headed by a Board consisting of ten people appointed by the minister responsible for DOE(NI). Included among the ten are the chairman and vice-chairman, both of whom the minister directly appoints. His choice of the remainder of Board members is constrained in a number of ways. Three Board members are councillors, selected by the Housing Council (which is described later). Given that these are invariably members of the two main Unionist parties (Official Unionist and Democratic Unionist), the minister usually appoints representatives from the two main non-unionist parties (the Alliance Party and the Social Democratic and Labour Party). In addition, he or she is required by the legislation to ensure that one of the Board appointees is a woman, and there are attempts to ensure that a tenant representative is included.

The parent Department of NIHE is the Northern Ireland

Department of the Environment (DOE [NI]). It has the right
to 'give directions of a general or specific nature to the Executive as to the manner in which it is to discharge its functions'
(Housing (NI) Order 1981 Art. 10). In addition, the DOE(NI)
has to approve such housing schemes as it requires to be submit-
ted, approve the declaration of clearance areas and redevelop-
ment areas, vesting of land and the declaration of housing
action areas.

With respect to finance, the Housing Finance Order (No.
597, [NI 8] 1977), updated by the Housing (NI) Order 1981,
provides the basic legislative framework. The Executive must
submit to DOE(NI), in such form as the Department may
direct, estimates of the income and expenditure of the Executive during the following financial year, and 'shall submit such
other information relating to these estimates as the Department
may require' (Article 18 [1], 1981 Housing Order).

The Department has a major say in each of the Executive's
main sources of income. The original complex system of grants,
which was a legacy from the pre–1973 local government system,
has been replaced by a single grant. According to the 1981
Order (s. 20, para. 1) the DOE(NI) may

> in respect of each financial year pay to the Executive at such
> times, in such manner and subject to such conditions as the
> Department may think fit, a grant towards the expenditure
> incurred or to be incurred by the Executive in that year.

The Executive has to submit to DOE(NI) the scheme for
determining the rent, and the Department may require the
Executive to amend that scheme. Further, the minister has the
power to direct the Executive to increase rents. In addition,
the Executive may, with the approval of the Department of
Finance and Personnel, borrow money for house-building purposes.

It was recognised also that local government had a particular
interest in housing matters and, it is involved formally in housing decision-making in a number of ways. At a policy level,
councils have been afforded entry to decision-making through
two institutional arrangements. Each of the twenty-six councils
are represented on the Housing Council, which gives policy

advice to NIHE and DOE(NI). In addition, as already stated, the Housing Council elects three out of the ten members of the Board of the Executive.

The Chief Executive of NIHE and appropriate colleagues attend a meeting of each council once a year to explain housing policy as it affects that district. This meeting is supposedly concerned with the new building programme, but other issues from general policy matters to the quality of the maintenance programme in the district can arise. A constant complaint from NIHE officials is that councillors invariably seem more interested in individual constituency matters than policy matters.

In general, councils, especially those dominated by Official Unionists and Democractic Unionists, feel that their views are not taken into account sufficiently by the Executive. This is due in part to the inability of the Executive to deliver all that is demanded of it by the councillors. More importantly, Unionists feel that the existence of NIHE is politically unacceptable, as it owes its origins to an analysis of housing problems in Northern Ireland that questions the record of the pre-1972 Unionist administration (Birrell 1981). In addition to these party political complaints, there is resentment in some rural councils that, as they see it, new housing development neglects rural areas. This view tends to cut across the sectarian divide, and is directed at the planning authorities rather than at the NIHE.

The third role of councillors in the housing policy network is that of mediator for individual (and sometimes groups of) constituents. A great deal of councillors' work is concerned with housing, despite their limited formal role, with constituents believing that councillor mediation with NIHE is useful. Thus, for councillors housing is a key issue on which they exercise what they perceive as too little influence.

Government by public agencies: policing and employment

When the violence of the late 1960s drew the British government more seriously into Northern Ireland politics, one of the first areas for reform was law and order. In August 1969 an inquiry into Northern Ireland's police forces, headed by Lord Hunt, was established. The Hunt Committee reported in October 1969 and recommended considerable changes in the management and operation of the police. Among the proposals were the replacement of the Ulster Special Constabulary (USC) by a new part-time security force, the Ulster Defence Regiment (UDR), the creation of a police authority representative of the whole community and the civilianisation of the Royal Ulster Constabulary (RUC). The various reforms were embodied in the Police Act (Northern Ireland) 1970. As indicated in the previous chapter, the continuing violence frustrated many of Hunt's recommendations, for example the disarming of RUC officers, but the Act provides the continuing basis of the government of the police, including the creation of the Police Authority for Northern Ireland.

The Police Authority for Northern Ireland

Section 1 of the Act established the Authority as a body corporate vested with the duty to secure the maintenance of an adequate and efficient police force. Its powers, like the role of the Chief Constable, were modelled on police authorities in England and Wales (Oliver 1987). The Authority has a responsibility to carry out several specific functions:

1. To determine the size and rank structure of the RUC.
2. To appoint all officers of the rank of Assistant Chief Constable and above.
3. To provide and maintain all buildings, equipment and supplies essential to the proper functioning of the RUC.
4. To keep itself informed as to the manner in which complaints from members of the public are dealt with by the Chief Constable.
5. To exercise financial and budgetary control of expenditure on police services.

The operational control and direction of the RUC is the independent responsibility of the Chief Constable. He has, for example, control over the disposition of his officers. He is not subject to direction on operational matters either by the Secretary of State for Northern Ireland or the Police Authority.

The Northern Ireland Office (NIO) also has financial and other responsibilities in this area. The Permanent Secretary at NIO is the accounting officer for the Police Authority. NIO has to ensure that the Police Authority spends its funds in a proper way. Securing the proper balance between the Authority, the Chief Constable and the Department is not easy.

The Authority consists of a chairman, a vice-chairman and between fourteen and twenty members, all appointed by the Secretary of State. There is an effort made to ensure that the Authority is 'representative' of the community at large, but in practice this has been difficult to achieve. PIRA has murdered two members of the Authority and issued statements threatening Catholics on the Authority. Consequently, there have been difficulties in ensuring that there is adequate cross-community representation. Recently, there has been an attempt to escape this difficulty by not providing the names of those on the Authority, but this raises questions of accountability.

On the whole, the dominant figures in policing in Northern Ireland have been the Chief Constable and the Secretary of State. In the main, the Authority is trapped between these two levels and plays a minor role. A variety of factors play a part in this situation, but the most significant one has been violence. In these circumstances, the professional judgement of the Chief Constable and the political support of the Secretary of State are the key elements and non-elected members have a limited role.

The Fair Employment Agency (FEA)

During the 1960s and early 1970s there were a number of attempts in Britain to use legislation to eliminate various types of discrimination, including racial and sexual discrimination. It was only natural that this approach would be adopted in Northern Ireland in an effort to eliminate religious and political discrimination. In 1972 the British government established a working party to

consider what steps, whether in regard to law or practice, should be taken to counter religious discrimination, whether it may exist in the private sector of employment in Northern Ireland. (MHSS 1973)

Its main recommendations were incorporated into the Fair Employment (Northern Ireland) Act 1976 (Mullen 1988a). This Act created the Fair Employment Agency (FEA), the purposes of which were to promote equality of opportunity and secure remedies for unlawful discrimination. Members of the Agency were appointed by the Department of Economic Development (DED) on the basis of recommendations from both sides of industry. The composition of the Agency was supposed to represent the religious divide of the community. DED provided the budget for the Agency and approved appointments to the staff of the Agency, a relationship that some saw as too close (Mullen 1988a).

The Act afforded individual redress against religious discrimination in the fields of governmental and public sector activity and public and private sector employment. It excluded private sector housing and the provision of goods and services (Osbourne 1981, p. 337). The legislation also excluded employment among school teachers. The FEA is also responsible for the promotion of equality of opportunity in employment between those of different religious beliefs.

The Agency had three main powers:

1. To investigate individual complaints.
2. To investigate employment practices to judge whether they accord with principles of equality of opportunity.
3. To monitor and research patterns and trends in occupations and employment.

Combating discrimination in employment is seen as important in solving the problems of Northern Ireland. It is an issue that has become even more politically important since the 1976 Act. In part this is due to the efforts of certain Irish-Americans to increase awareness about employment patterns between the religious groups in Northern Ireland among US companies that are considering investing in Northern Ireland.

Attention is focused on the so-called McBride principles.

These are a nine-point anti-discrimination code of behaviour, co-sponsored by Sean McBride, one-time minister in the Irish government and Nobel Peace Prize winner (Osbourne and Cormack 1989). For example, the McBride principles include special recruitment efforts to attract applicants from under-represented religious groups. The principles were modelled on those of the Sullivan code of conduct, which was aimed at ending discrimination in South Africa.

In addition, a number of studies, in particular one carried out by the Policy Studies Institute on behalf of the Standing Advisory Commission on Human Rights, added to the pressure on government. This study was published in 1987 and entitled 'Equality and inequality in Northern Ireland'. It confirmed, as did a number of other studies sponsored by the FEA, that discrimination was still a major problem in Northern Ireland (Osbourne and Cormack 1989).

The Fair Employment Commission (FEC)

The 1976 legislation and the FEA were seen to be inadequate in a number of respects. A number of critics (Graham 1983; McCrudden 1983; Mullen 1988a and 1988b) accused the FEA of being timid in its approach. McCrudden, for example, argued that the FEA totally failed to meet the challenge it faced, and recommended a complete overhaul of the Agency. Barry White's judgement was that 'although progress has been made in some fields – notably in companies like Shorts which have been the subject of FEA investigation – the overall employment picture is little changed since the early 1970s' (White 1986, p. 9). White suggests that one of the key problems has been a lack of resources, and Osbourne has described the Agency as a 'modest "quango" in terms of manpower and expenditure' (Osbourne 1981, p. 338).

The various pressures persuaded the Department of Economic Development to publish, in 1988, new proposals to amend the legislation. The new legislation came into effect from 1990. Central to it is the replacement of the FEA by a Fair Employment Commission which takes over the FEA's staff and assets. The FEC is given the power to investigate and audit employment practices and direct the 'affirmative' action to be taken. Investigation of individual complaints of discrimination are to be dealt with by a new Fair Employment Tribunal. The Act also explicitly outlaws indirect discrimination. There is also compulsory monitoring for all public sector employers and private sector employers with twenty-five or more employees (to be reduced to ten after two years). Failure to monitor is a criminal offence.

The FEA therefore has been replaced by a more powerful organisation, reflecting the government's concern to end job discrimination based on religion. It is probably true to say that the FEA played a part in its own demise by supplying information that it was not succeeding and that additional powers were required. What happens to the FEC and whether it achieves its aims will be interesting to observe.

Northern Ireland government

Macrory had predicated his reforms on the continued existence of a Parliament at Stormont. In this way, he argued, democratic accountability could be maintained, with regional services being held accountable to the regional Parliament and local services to elected local authorities. Instead, because of the continuing violence, Stormont was prorogued on 24 March 1972. Since then, Northern Ireland has been governed through a Secretary of State, who is a member of the United Kingdom Cabinet, and is assisted by several ministers (originally two Ministers of State and one Parliamentary Under Secretary, now with an additional Parliamentary Under Secretary). The government ministers with responsibility for Northern Ireland in the Spring of 1990 are shown in Table 5.2.

The role of the Secretary of State

The Secretary of State is charged with representing Northern Ireland's interests in the Cabinet, particularly, as the 1973 NI Constitutional Act states, in relation to the allocation of financial resources. Merlyn Rees (1980) has revealed that, except in

times of crises, Northern Ireland does not loom large in the
Cabinet's considerations:

> The main work is left to the Northern Ireland Committee of the
> Cabinet under whatever name successive governments give it.
> In practice, the responsibility falls almost completely to the
> Secretary of State allied closely with the Secretary of State for
> Defence.

Table 5.2 Government ministers in Northern Ireland

The Spring 1990 ministerial team were as follows:

Peter Brooke	Secretary of State.
John Cope	Deputy to Secretary of State and Minister responsible for Finance and Personnel as well as Law and Order.
Lord Skelmersdale	Spokesman for Northern Ireland in the House of Lords, Minister responsible for DHSS
Brian Mawhinney	Under-Secretary, Minister responsible for Education, Political Affairs Division and Information Services
Richard Needham	Under-Secretary, Minister responsible for DED and urban renewal activities of DOE
Peter Bottomley	Under-Secretary, Minister responsible for Dept of Agriculture and activities of DOE other than urban renewal, with particular emphasis on transport.

This gives to the Secretary of State a range of responsibilities
that are much greater than either his Scottish or Welsh counterparts. Roy Mason, a former Secretary of State, once told a
radio interviewer that he regarded himself, in presiding over a
team of ministers and departments, as a mini-prime minister
(quoted in Bell 1987, pp. 191–2).

The 1974 Northern Ireland Act made the Secretary of State

responsible for devolved services, with all power of executive government placed under his control.

> Under direct rule . . . the Secretary of State is responsible to Parliament for the efficient conduct of government by all . . . Northern Ireland Departments. However, what happens in practice is . . . (that) the Secretary of State delegates responsibility for the day-to-day administration of the Departments to ministers.
> (John Patten, Under-Secretary of State for Northern Ireland, *House of Commons Debates*, col. 1103, 8 April 1982)

The junior ministers are given responsibility for one or two departments. In addition, they are also asked to have a special concern for certain areas reserved to the Secretary of State, that is, those matters coming directly under the responsibility of the Northern Ireland Office and the Department of Finance and Personnel.

The introduction of Direct Rule in 1972 was seen as a temporary measure until a restructured devolved government could be secured. However, this short-term expedient has lasted longer than anticipated. All British governments since 1972 have stated their desire to see an agreed system of devolved government in Northern Ireland. In some senses, therefore, an arrangement exists which is supposed to be temporary but which in practice appears to be the way in which Northern Ireland is likely to be governed for the foreseeable future.

The combination of Direct Rule as temporary expedient and permanent reality has affected the administrative framework in a number of ways. For one thing the Secretary of State has taken a greater interest in the devolved services. He still has the responsibility to secure a political settlement. All Secretaries of State have taken political initiatives in an effort to resolve the position in Northern Ireland, even if the suspicion has been that not all of them wholeheartedly believed that they were likely to succeed. The need for the Secretary of State to be neutral in order to undertake this task has meant that, unlike his Scottish and Welsh counterparts, no person from Northern Ireland has been appointed as Secretary of State and, up to

the present time, only one – Brian Mawhinney – has been
appointed in any ministerial capacity.

Governmental machinery

The administrative arrangements to support the Secretary of
State for Northern Ireland and his colleagues are unique in
certain respects. At central government level his officials are
divided between Northern Ireland and Whitehall civil servants.
The Northern Ireland Civil Service (NICS) came into existence
as a result of the Ministries (NI) Act 1921 to administer those
functions which had been devolved to Northern Ireland by
Westminster under the Government of Ireland Act 1920. The
NICS is, *inter alia*, responsible for administering the Northern
Ireland Departments (NIDs), the origins of which also go back
to the 1921 Act mentioned above. This Act created seven
ministries in all, including a Prime Minister's Department, each
of which was a legal entity in its own right. The Act also defined
the role of each of the departments and their relationship with
each other.

Major changes in the departmental arrangements were rare
until Direct Rule. In 1940 a Ministry of Public Security
emerged, but it only lasted for the duration of the war. In 1944
Home Affairs was split, with some functions going to a new
Ministry of Health and Local Government. In 1964 this Ministry and the Ministry of Labour were abolished and their responsibilities divided into two departments, Health and Social Services, and Development. In 1969, a Ministry of Community
Relations came into existence. Hence by 1972 there existed
four of the original departments (the Prime Minister's Office,
Finance, Commerce and Agriculture), two slimmed-down ministries (Home Affairs and Education) and three 'new' departments (Health and Social Services, Development and Community Relations), making a total of nine in all.

These departments operated to a significant degree in isolation from each other. Birrell and Murie (1980) concluded
that despite the smallness of the region and the administrative
machinery, 'co-operation and co-ordination appeared to present more difficulties than might have been expected' (p. 142).

They argue that the replication of the Westminster model meant that Stormont imported some of the rigidities of the larger system. Further, some Stormont departments tended to look to their Westminster equivalent as their source of policy initiatives, rather than developing a more integrated approach with other Northern Ireland ministries. In addition there was less mobility among Northern Ireland civil servants than their Westminster counterparts. Northern Ireland civil servants often stayed within one department throughout their careers, a practice which made it more difficult to see the points of view of other departments.

The Stormont administration had three main links with Whitehall. First, Northern Ireland matters were the responsibility of the Home Office. These did not, however, merit a high priority within that department. As James Callaghan (1973, p. 2) points out:

> Northern Ireland was dealt with by the General Department of the Home Office, a body which covered such matters as ceremonial functions, British Summer Time, London taxi cabs, liquor licensing, the administration of state-owned pubs in Carlisle, and the protection of animals and birds. One division also dealt with the Channel Islands, the Isle of Man, the Charity Commission and Northern Ireland, and this group of subjects was under the control of a staff of seven, of whom only one was a member of what was called the administrative class.

The major concern of the Home Office in relation to Northern Ireland was to ensure a smooth working relationship with Stormont.

Second, financial relationships were, in essence, the subject of negotiation between the Treasury and the then Northern Ireland Ministry of Finance. In 1938 the principle of parity of service provision for citizens in Northern Ireland with those in the rest of the United Kingdom was established. In 1942 it was recognised that Northern Ireland had 'leeway' to make up in order to attain British standards. By 1950 an expenditure system based on an assessment of local needs had been established (Green 1979, pp. 14–19). The Treasury was content with this arrangement in that the Northern Ireland Department of Finance had a Treasury-type relationship with the other departments. Once the global sums had been agreed, the Treasury could then leave matters in the hands of the Department of Finance, confident that expenditure would be properly scrutinised.

Third, specific departments had various contacts with relevant Westminster departments. The Department of Agriculture (NI) in particular has had a long tradition of close links with its Whitehall counterpart, due to the fact that Northern Ireland's Agriculture is big enough to be significant in the United Kingdom context.

Central government under Direct Rule

As Direct Rule has continued, a change has occurred in the relationship between the Northern Ireland Office and the Northern Ireland departments. As pointed out earlier, the Northern Ireland departments have distinctive legal and cultural traditions, with NICS a separate civil service from the Home (that is, Whitehall) Civil Service. It therefore is not surprising that relationships between the Northern Ireland Office, staffed partly by Home civil servants, and the Northern Ireland departments staffed by NICS have not been completely harmonious, particularly at the start of Direct Rule.

Northern Ireland departments focused on their traditional policy areas. The initial outcome was poor co-ordination, which gradually, as Direct Rule continued, was countered. For example, secondment from NICS to the UK Civil Service, particularly to the Northern Ireland Office in London, has increased. The initial resentment felt by NICS officials towards London civil servants has been greatly diminished, in part because the Northern Ireland government is now more enmeshed into the Whitehall machinery. NICS appreciates the value of the skills and expertise of UK civil servants in dealing with Whitehall and Westminster. This has helped NICS to overcome differences in law and administration, as well as practice, and has enabled Northern Ireland civil servants involved in policy-making to keep up with changes in Whitehall.

An important development since 1972 has been the various efforts made to improve the machinery of government. Shortly after Direct Rule, a Policy Co-ordination Committee, chaired by the Head of NICS, was created, with the task of reconciling inter-departmental conflict and considering issues of an inter-departmental nature. The role of this Committee has developed and more attention has been given to the problem of policy co-ordination.

In 1976 a separate post of Head of NICS, and second Permanent Secretary at the NIO, was created. This person was made directly responsible to the Secretary of State for the co-ordination of the policies and programmes of all Northern Ireland departments, the general management of the NICS and recommendations to top appointments (Birrell and Murie 1980, p. 152). Northern Ireland civil servants would argue that there is now much improved co-ordination between departments. To quote one: '. . . partly because of the high quality of its co-ordinating machinery, Northern Ireland in its dealings with Whitehall and Brussels can get its act together well ahead of other regions' (private correspondence with author).

Since Direct Rule the number and functions of the Northern Ireland departments have also been altered. There have been two major phases of restructuring. The first in 1974, was intended to secure sufficient ministerial posts to sustain the Power-Sharing Executive. The second, in 1975, was designed to enable the Secretary of State and his ministers to pursue their policies more effectively and efficiently. This latter reorganisation saw the separation of the Department of the Civil Service from the Department of Finance in 1976.

As in Whitehall, this decision was subsequently revised and, under the Departments (NI) Order 1982 (Art. 1, 1982 [338 NI 6]), the Department of Finance was retitled the Department of Finance and Personnel (DFP) and the Department of the Civil Service was dissolved and its functions transferred to the retitled Department. In addition, various functions of the DFP were transferred to other departments. The purpose of this change was to create a department 'responsible for resource planning across the range of functions exercised by all Northern Ireland Departments' (Mr J. Patten, Under-Secretary of State for Northern Ireland, Debate on the Draft Departments (NI) Order, *House of Commons Debates*, col. 944, 24 February 1982). Further, the departments concerned with economic development, namely Commerce and Manpower Services, were merged to form the Department of Economic Development. These changes, together with the fact that the NIO has taken over the Ministry of Home Affairs, means that there are currently six Northern Ireland departments:

1. Finance and Personnel.
2. Economic Development.
3. Environment.
4. Education.
5. Health and Social Services.
6. Agriculture.

The Northern Ireland Office is responsible for law and order services, as well as general advice to the Secretary of State on the overall political situation. It is headed by a permanent secretary drawn from the Home Civil Service.

Parliament and Northern Ireland

Given the importance of central government in the affairs of Northern Ireland, it might be thought that the Westminster Parliament would become a vital arena for ensuring that public servants and ministers are accountable for their actions. In this regard Scotland, with a local government system with considerably more powers than that in Northern Ireland, might provide a model.

The 1979 House of Commons Redistribution of Seats Act increased the number of Northern Ireland MPs from twelve to seventeen. The argument for this was the absence of a devolved Parliament. Within Northern Ireland, the decision was welcomed by the main Unionist parties and the Alliance Party but opposed by the Nationalist parties.

Given the absence of devolved government in Northern Ireland, Westminster has had to find time to discuss the whole range of its affairs. It has also had to find a way of ensuring that legislation affecting Northern Ireland is satisfactorily processed.

In solving these problems the temporary nature of Direct Rule has greatly influenced matters. Excepted matters are dealt with through the normal parliamentary process and the bills which pass through Parliament are known as Acts. There is, however, no Northern Ireland equivalent of the Scottish Grand Committee or Scottish Standing Committees. Hence the Northern Ireland input to Northern Ireland legislation is less than the contribution of Scottish MPs to Scottish legislation.

Under the 1974 Act, those matters that were transferred or reserved are legislated by Order in Council. Orders in Council are not subject to the scrutiny of Parliament to the same degree or in the same way as is ordinary legislation. Delegated legislation cannot be amended by Parliament. It is either accepted or rejected in its entirety.

The 1974 Act provides that Orders in Council for Northern Ireland are made once 'a draft of the Order has been approved by resolution of each House'. 'This is commonly known as the affirmative procedure and requires the government to ensure that time is made available to each House for it to consider the draft and then to approve (or reject) it' (Hadfield 1990). There is also a negative procedure, under which a draft order will come into force unless within forty sitting days of its being laid one or both Houses votes against it. This procedure has been used for Northern Ireland legislation when it is virtually identical to legislation which has been introduced into the rest of the United Kingdom.

The government recognised that parliamentary scrutiny for Northern Ireland legislation was unsatisfactory and has made some attempts at improving matters. It introduced a proposal for a draft Order. In this case, the government circulates to interested persons the legislative proposal and invites comments, to which it can react if it so desires. This is a pre-parliamentary procedure that introduces some flexibility into the system.

Since 1975 there has been a Northern Ireland Committee of the House of Commons, which is a Standing Committee of the House and consists of all the Northern Ireland MPs and up to twenty-five others. This Committee considers matters on Northern Ireland referred to it by the government. The Committee has not been a success and indeed has not been used to any great extent. This is partly because it only discusses what the government wishes it to, and partly because it can only recommend changes to the government.

With respect to controlling the work of the executive branch, there are three aspects of Parliament's work that merit attention. First, the Secretary of State and his ministerial colleagues are, like other ministers, subject to parliamentary questions. Second, Northern Ireland matters are, on various occasions, debated on the floor of the House. Finally, the Select Committees of the House, particularly the Public Accounts Committee, investigate aspects of the government of Northern Ireland. For example, the Energy Committee investigated the proposals to privatise Northern Ireland Electricity and produced a report in November 1987. One of the earliest, and for many years the only, example was the investigation by the Select Committee on Education into Further and Higher Education in Northern Ireland, which produced a report in 1983.

There remains the question of whether these are adequate mechanisms of control and accountability. In general, many people within Northern Ireland, particularly in the unionist community, would think not. While matters have improved greatly, the workings of the Northern Ireland departments are rarely subject to serious scrutiny. Certainly compared with the scrutiny afforded under the Assembly between 1982 and 1986, the extent of parliamentary scrutiny is very limited (O'Leary et al. 1988). Given that local government is so limited, this low level of investigation is even more serious. This also raises the problem that many in Northern Ireland feel that they have relatively little influence over the legislation and decisions that are made in their name.

Conclusion: taking administration out of politics – at a price

The various reforms since the early 1970s have radically altered governmental structures within Northern Ireland. Table 5.1 indicates the major institutions responsible for particular services. There are clear and obvious differences between the structure in Northern Ireland and in the rest of the United Kingdom. In Northern Ireland, local authorities have executive responsibility for fewer services and there is a much greater attempt to take services 'out of politics' through the use of non-elected public bodies.

This attempt to depoliticise services has partially succeeded in that fewer charges of discrimination are heard. But the action of the public bodies continues to generate political debate. Councillors feel frustrated that they can only voice complaints and act as a lobby, instead of controlling services directly. The system encourages councillors to act 'irresponsibly': to simply attack the public agencies.

There is little political capital to be made from attempting to justify or explain the decision of such agencies. Indeed it is not unknown for councillors to participate in a decision of a public agency through membership of a board and then to attack it in the council or some other public platform. This, in turn, causes officials to denigrate politicians and accuse them of irresponsibility. There is therefore a built-in tension within the system.

This tension is additional to the underlying social conflict which was the major force in changing the system. There were, of course, concerns about the efficiency and effectiveness of local institutions: concerns which were similar in many ways to those in Britain. But the debate in Northern Ireland about institutions – and their reforms – owed more to the dynamics of local politics than anything else.

Since the new institutions were created, changes have occurred as people have attempted to work with what were perceived to be temporary institutions. The attempt to end Direct Rule has so far failed, and both ministers and civil servants have tried to make adjustments within the system to render it more efficient and responsive. In addition, it has been brought more into the Whitehall system. This has increased the obvious trend of removing responsibility from local institutions to Westminster and from politicians to administrators.

In this way, an effort has been made to manage the Northern Ireland problem by attempting to depoliticise issues. Because of this, public officials – whether they are civil servants, local government officers or professionals – have grown in importance at the expense of politicians, particularly local politicians.

6

Political Groupings in Northern Ireland

This chapter describes the main political groupings in Northern Ireland and in so doing seeks to find insights into the politics of the territory. As is clear, these are characterised by a high degree of polarisation. Phrases such as 'bipolar political society', 'governing without consensus' and 'ideological style of political discourse' have been used to describe the strongly conflictual nature of politics within Northern Ireland (Arthur 1984; Bew *et al.* 1979; Birrell and Murie 1980; Rose 1971, 1976). The polarisation takes place around two competing ideologies, namely unionism and nationalism, and it is these deeply-felt and mutually-exclusive ideologies that give Northern Irish politics its distinctive nature.

The basic political divide

The basic issue behind these ideologies is the constitutional position of Northern Ireland within the United Kingdom. Unionists support Northern Ireland remaining a part of the United Kingdom, while Nationalists are in favour of closer ties or even its union with the rest of Ireland. The conflict is further heightened in that this political cleavage coincides almost exactly with a religious division, Protestants being unionist and Catholics nationalist.

The depth of this political division is indicated by the fact that approximately 90 per cent of the votes cast in elections will be for parties firmly committed to these ideological positions, as shown in Table 6.1. Stronger evidence of the passions generated by politics in Northern Ireland is, of course, the prolonged violence, which in recent years has seen over 2,750 people killed, many more injured, and considerable intimidation of people in their homes and, to a lesser extent, at work.

Despite this political polarisation it is an oversimplification to describe Northern Ireland purely in terms of two rigid camps. Both communities have groups with different commitments to, and understandings of, these ideologies. There is also evidence that some issues cut across the central division in society. Class co-operation on specific and limited issues has taken place on occasions. For example, Devlin (1981) writes about Catholic and Protestant workers joining together to oppose aspects of government policy in the 1920s and 1930s.

In addition there are a number of small political parties – principally the Alliance party and the Workers Party – which make efforts to appeal to both sides. These may help to restrain the major division in some circumstances. Indeed, while Northern Ireland is often spoken about in terms of this central division there are some writers who, while accepting its reality, argue that 'there are factors which regulate and limit the conflict' (Darby 1985, p. 82).

Paradoxically, while a key element in the basic division is the argument about the British link, it might be argued that it is one of the major constraining factors. Considerable public expenditure has been employed to reduce economic and social deprivation. Without these funds, it is likely that the position would be a good deal worse. Some of the implications are examined later, but it is important to remember that politics in Northern Ireland are more complex than they are often presented.

Despite these caveats, however, there remains the basic political divide, and it is important to examine the main political groupings within each community. Arthur (1984, p. 52) points out that, since 1970, some ten new political parties have emerged, some with a short life-span. The focus here will be on the five main political groupings: the two main unionist

Table 6.1 Election results in Northern Ireland: 1975–87 (%)

The electoral performance of political parties in Northern Ireland

	OUP %	DUP %	Other Unionist %	Alliance %	SDLP %	Sinn Fein %	Other Nationalist %	WP %	NILP %	CP %	Other %
1975 Convention election	25.8	14.8	21.9	9.8	23.7	–	–	2.2	1.4	0.1	0.3
1979 General election	36.6	10.2	12.3	11.9	19.7	–	6.5	1.7	0.6	–	0.5
1979 European election	21.9	29.8	7.3	6.8	24.6	–	5.9	0.8	–	–	2.9
1982 Assembly election	29.7	23.0	5.7	9.3	18.8	10.1	–	2.7	–	–	0.7
1983 General election	34.0	20.0	3.1	8.0	17.9	13.4	–	2.0	–	–	1.6
1984 European election	21.5	33.6	2.9	5.0	22.1	13.3	–	1.3	–	–	0.3
1985 Local government election	29.5	24.3	3.1	10.0	21.1	11.4	2.4	1.6	–	–	2.4
1987 General election	37.9	11.7	5.3	10.0	21.1	11.4	–	2.6	–	–	–
1989 Local government election	30.4	18.7	3.8	6.9	21.0	11.2	–	2.1	–	–	4.9

Source: Irish Times, and the Electoral Office for Northern Ireland
Note: OUP = Official Unionist Party; DUP = Democratic Unionist Party; SDLP = Social Democratic and Labour Party (includes independent SDLP in 1979 general election); WP = Workers' Party (formerly Republican Clubs); NILP = Northern Ireland Labour Party; CP = Communist Party

parties, Official Unionist Party (OUP) and the Democratic Unionist Party (DUP); the main nationalist party, the Social Democratic and Labour Party (SDLP); the main Republican party, Sinn Fein; and the Alliance Party, which though a unionist party attempts to appeal to both traditions within Northern Ireland. In addition, the main paramilitary groupings, the Ulster Defence Association (UDA) and the Ulster Volunteer Force (UVF) on the loyalist side, and the Irish Republican Army (IRA) on the republican side, will be discussed.

Two varieties of Unionism

While the principal tenet of Unionism is that the constitutional link with Britain should be preserved, there are a number of disparate elements in the political ideology of Unionism (Rose 1971; Todd 1987; Wallis *et al.* 1986; Wright 1973). Todd (1987) distinguishes between *Ulster Loyalist* and *Ulster British* ideologies. She argues that the essential characteristics of '*Ulster Loyalist*' ideology are that its *primary* identification is as Northern Protestant while its identification with Britain involves only *secondary* loyalty. She claims that it derives its essential nature from the evangelical fundamentalist religious tradition, and that its core assumption is that the only alternative to Ulster loyalist dominance is Ulster loyalist defeat and humiliation (Todd 1987, p. 3).

As Moloney and Pollock (1986, p. 434) put it: 'Defeat would mean an all-Ireland Republic, and the spiritual and political slavery of Catholicism.' This notion of struggle – an inevitable struggle – with the forces of evil has often meant that the compromiser is to be suspected and it is vitally important to keep the chosen people secure and separate. Within this tradition, loyalty to Britain is conditional on the Protestantism of the monarch and on the British government dealing fairly with Ulster.

Frank Wright (1973) suggests a similar division, distinguishing between an extreme and a moderate or liberal Unionism. The extreme faction argue that Roman Catholicism is implacably opposed to the existence of a Northern Ireland state and, therefore, that 'concessions to particular socio-economic demands of Catholics (for example, over jobs and housing discrimination) will in no way soften their political or religious hostility to Ulster' (Wright 1973, p. 237). 'Any Catholic or Nationalist self-assertion is seen as a stain on the Protestant ethos of the society and as an opening for bloody Republican rebellion' (Dewar *et al.* 1969 in Todd 1987, p. 7). For many loyalists, there is a great strength to be drawn from past victories against 'Romanism and Republicanism'. Carson's stand and victory against Home Rule is often quoted.

Todd (1987, p. 11) states that the imagined community within the *'Ulster British'* ideology is Greater Britain, although within this there is a secondary regional identification with Northern Ireland. Unionists in this tradition – as with Wright's 'Liberal Unionist' – identify with the British parliamentary traditions, and generally disapprove of sectarianism. Certainly they are deeply uneasy with some of the wilder expressions of anti-Catholicism. They would also be more willing to engage in rational discussion about the merits of the Union, citing, for example, pragmatic considerations such as the quality of economic life and the Welfare State.

The unionist political parties

The extreme ideological position is represented by the Official Unionist Party (OUP) and the Democratic Unionist Party (DUP). While there is strong competition between the two parties for votes they hold a broadly similar political stance. Birrell and Murie (1980, p. 102) have argued that this contains four main elements:

1. Rejection of a united Ireland.
2. The maintenance of the border.
3. The continuance of the Northern Ireland State and the union with Great Britain.
4. The political ascendency of the Unionists.

Both parties tend to argue for a strong security policy. They believe that 'a political solution' (which means, in practice, compromise with those they see as Ulster's enemies) is difficult if not unacceptable.

In addition both parties tend to distrust British government attitudes towards Northern Ireland and wish to see devolved government restored so that the future will again be in the hands of the loyalist majority. This view is more strongly held within the DUP.

Both main Unionist parties, and the majority of the unionist community, are deeply hostile to the Republic of Ireland. On the whole they see it as an alien society, dominated by the Catholic clergy and desirous of taking over Northern Ireland. Sarah Nelson reports that those UDA 'officers' she interviewed saw the Republic of Ireland as anti-British and anti-Protestant. 'It insulted all the symbols they respected and the things with which they were familiar' (Nelson 1984, p. 113). Unionists see the territorial claims enshrined in the Constitution of the Republic as a fundamental source of offence. It prolongs the violence because it identifies both the government of the Republic of Ireland and the Provisional IRA as seeking a united Ireland (O'Malley 1983, p. 134).

Both the OUP and DUP have also considerable reservations about the role of the Catholic Church in political affairs. Suspicions stretch from a concern about specific issues, for example the view that the Catholic Church's desire to sustain a separate education system is divisive, to a general attitude that all things Catholic are suspect.

(A) The Democratic Unionist Party (DUP)

This latter philosophy is held strongly within the DUP, which was formed by Ian Paisley in September 1971. At that time there was some talk of uniting anti-Faulkner Unionists into a single political party. However, Paisley pre-empted this with an announcement that he was going to form the DUP. While it is likely that this was a long-term strategy, the immediate announcement came after an IRA bomb exploded in a public house on the loyalist Shankill Road (Moloney and Pollock 1986, p. 267).

The DUP tends to take a more extreme view than the Official Unionist Party. In part, this stems from the close identification of the DUP with fundamentalist protestant sects, particularly Dr Paisley's Free Presbyterian Church, which are often strongly anti-Roman Catholic. The DUP usually supports such issues as closing of leisure centres on Sundays. It is also influenced by the fact that the OUP formed the government of Northern Ireland for approximately fifty years. The DUP came into existence as a result of disaffection with the actions of OUP ministers (Nelson 1984; Moloney and Pollock 1986). The DUP was to some extent a party of the disaffected among the unionist community. It tends to thrive during periods of unionist crisis. As Moloney and Pollock (1986, p. 265) put it: 'The DUP vote has become a barometer of Protestant angst.'

The DUP remains dominated by Dr Paisley's strong personality. His physical presence and his ability to articulate the fears of many Unionists with a memorable, sometimes witty, phrase have made him a dominant figure in Northern Ireland's politics for the past twenty years (An example of his wit was when he replied to Terence O'Neill's remarks that he was engaged in bridge-building by declaring that the one thing a bridge and a traitor had in common was to cross over to the other side! (quoted in Arthur 1984, p. 94)). Many members of the Party believe that he is chosen by God to protect Ulster, and hence are reluctant to oppose him. Attacks on him by the media or other politicians on the whole do not affect his popularity. Indeed, they are taken as a sign of his integrity and the perfidious nature of his detractors. Those within the Party who attempt to generate alternative policies to him generally either have to come into line or leave (Smyth 1987). None the less, in recent years there has occurred a new influx into the DUP, a more secularised and well-educated group led by people such as Peter Robinson, MP for East Belfast, and Sammy Wilson, formerly Lord Mayor of Belfast.

(B) The Official Unionist Party (OUP)

The OUP traces its origins to the old Unionist Party that dominated Northern Ireland's politics for so long (Harbinson 1973). The Party was virtually unchallenged on the unionist side and its influence was felt in all aspects of life in Northern Ireland from 1922 onwards. This apparently monolithic structure eventually broke up under the pressures of having to come to terms with the civil rights movement and greater British 'interference'. Many Unionists found it hard to accept London's new involvement in Northern Ireland's affairs. Essentially, the OUP represents the remnants of the Unionist Party that refused to accede to the various reform proposals.

The OUP is closely intertwined with the Orange Order. Traditionally members of the Party were also members of the Order. Indeed this was one of the areas of concern expressed by Nationalists in general about the Unionist Party. The Order was also used to protect the Party against dissenting Protestants. For example, the Order made sure that Free Presbyterian ministers could not be chaplains of Orange lodges, a position that would provide them with considerable influence and aid the growth of Paisleyism (Moloney and Pollock 1986, pp. 51–2).

Currently, the OUP tends to have within its ranks a greater range of opinion than the DUP. For example, there are those within the Party who argue for integration with Britain. Additionally, some Official Unionists support the notion of a devolution on the basis of an agreed role for the Catholic community. But both of these are minority positions within the Party.

An important difference between the two parties is in the realm of personality – many Official Unionists find the personality of Dr Paisley a difficult one. Dr Paisley has attacked establishment figures in Unionism over a considerable number of years (Bruce 1986; Moloney and Pollock 1986). Moloney and Pollock argue that

> almost at the very start of his career he had the three pillars of the Protestant establishment (that is Orangeism, Unionism and Presbyterianism) lined up against him and he against them. The rest of his career would be dominated by the battle between them. (Moloney and Pollock 1986, p. 55)

Recent disagreements between the unionist parties

An example of the tensions between the main unionist parties can be seen in their reactions to the entry of Sinn Fein into electoral politics, and to the Anglo-Irish Agreement. Both parties fiercely resented both, but how to oppose them was a crucial issue. A great deal of protest took place in local government, as well as on the streets. One important dimension to the protests therefore was focused on the role that local government should play in the unionist campaign.

Withdrawing from local government would constitute a powerful expression of dissent. On the other hand, a complete withdrawal could mean a major confrontation with the British government, possible involvement with loyalist paramilitaries and a danger of greatly increased violence. Further, many Official Unionist councillors have a strong tradition of support for established institutions – they were after all the ruling elite within Northern Ireland for a considerable time. In addition, there is still a tradition among some councillors that local government is about community service, and they are uneasy about party politics in this area.

In the main the DUP have been less willing to compromise and more willing to engage in conflict with central government than the OUP. It is dangerous to generalise, as there are many in the ranks of the OUP equally entrenched as those in the DUP, but on the whole the OUP would tend to a less militant position. In many cases it was the OUP councillors who adopted the more moderate position. For example, they were more willing to comply with legal requirements. In North Down Council, a strongly OUP council, Unionists voted to resume normal business in direct contradiction to party policy. The 'rebel' Unionists argued that the adjournment tactic had run its course, its propaganda value had diminished, the machinery of local government had continued to operate and a number of councils still theoretically engaged in boycotts had been meeting to discuss selective business (Connolly and Knox 1988).

Councillors from both parties were also divided on the tactic of mass resignation. DUP councillors approved a policy of joint resignation if the two leaders gave the go-ahead and their councillors in Castlereagh led the way by placing their written resignations in the hands of the Mayor (Peter Robinson), a move designed to pressure OUP councillors.

Among Official Unionists there was a measure of unease about this course of action, partly because they perceived significant difficulties for some of the unionist-controlled councils as a result. If, after resignations, a council was left with a quorum (one-quarter of the total number of councillors, according to the 1972 Local Government Act), it could either co-opt new members or proceed to by-elections. In the absence of a quorum government-appointed commissioners would make council decisions.

Broadly, the DUP argued against ending the adjournment policy, even for tactical reasons, as this would weaken their protest against the Agreement. The OUP on the other hand felt they had lost control of the protest and had not intended to come into conflict with the courts.

By the 1989 local government elections the mood had swung in favour of the OUP. In that election they improved their position relative to the DUP, and took that as a sign that their more measured approach had electoral approval. By early 1990 most councils were working normally, but the OUP, with the DUP, still persisted in stating that they would not engage in political talks with the British government or other political parties until the Anglo-Irish Agreement was suspended.

The loyalist paramilitaries

In addition to the political parties, Protestant paramilitaries play a part in extreme Unionism, though they have never had the significant role of the Republican paramilitaries. In the main this is due to the different position of the two communities in relation to the state. But Protestant paramilitaries have played an important role at key moments. During the 1974 Workers' Strike, the Ulster Defence Association (UDA), the largest loyalist paramilitary organisation, had a significant impact on the success of the strike. On other occasions some unionist politicians have created alliances with loyalist paramilitaries.

One of the striking paradoxes has been the political initiatives which the UDA have advanced (Arthur and Jeffrey 1988). For example, in January 1987 the UDA published *Common Sense*, which among other things suggested power-sharing. *Common Sense* was radically different from the thinking of two main unionist parties, which were somewhat critical of the UDA's paper, but which felt sufficiently vulnerable to set up a 'task force' to produce their own paper.

There are a number of Protestant paramilitary groupings, the most prominent of which are the UDA and the UVF. The latter is the more violent and hardline, while the UDA is the larger. The UDA has been adversely affected by a number of allegations linking some of its leaders to attempts to secure monies for themselves. Both organisations remain powerful forces in Northern Ireland society and cannot be discounted.

The Alliance Party

Most political parties in Northern Ireland are what is referred to as 'confessional parties', that is, they aspire to 'religious exclusiveness and class inclusiveness' (McAllister 1983, p. 62). As McAllister (1983, p. 62) says, the main parties have everything to gain from exacerbating the religious cleavage, while 'concomitantly muting intra-communal differences such as class', to ensure the maximum support within their community. There are nevertheless a number of political parties which are bi-confessional, that is, they aspire to appeal across the communal divide. The Northern Ireland Labour and Liberal Parties were examples before the 1960s. More recently, the Alliance Party is the principal party which fits this description.

The Party was formed from the convergence of Captain O'Neill's supporters in the Unionist Party, the remnants of the Liberal Party and moderate Unionists associated with the New Ulster Movement, a non-party pressure group formed to support O'Neill's policies. The Alliance Party usually obtains between 7 and 10 per cent of the vote, drawn from both sides of the community. Indeed, given the levels of violence in Northern Ireland since 1970 it is a tribute to the party that it has retained this level of support. It is drawn mainly from the middle and upper socio-economic groups, particularly in the Greater Belfast area. Its ability to attract Catholic voters indicates that there are members of this community who are in favour of the maintenance of the Union. They could not support the other unionist parties, because these parties were identified with sectarianism.

The Alliance Party favours a Northern Ireland solution, based on power-sharing. It has been prepared to work with parties from both sides of the divide. It participated with the SDLP and moderate Unionists during the Power-Sharing Executive, when its leader held a Cabinet office. During the days of the Assembly it worked with the OUP and DUP. Its importance in Northern Ireland is greater than its voting strength as the Alliance Party is the furthermost point that some members of each community are prepared to move towards the other community. Its record ensures that it has a measure of trust from both sides.

Two varieties of Nationalism

The Roman Catholic minority generally supports some form of Irish Nationalism. This begins with the assertion that Northern Ireland should not be part of the United Kingdom, but united politically with the rest of Ireland. The clear implication is that the governmental arrangements for Northern Ireland are, in some measure, illegitimate and, for that reason, most Nationalists feel some degree of disaffection with the state.

This, together with their status as a permanent minority, has dominated the approach of Nationalists to politics. Many Catholics feel that they have not been treated fairly in the Northern Ireland state. For example, in Richard Rose's (1971) survey some 73 per cent of Catholics agreed with the statement that 'Catholics had been treated unfairly'. They believe that they have suffered discrimination of a political, psychological and economic nature.

These attitudes have shaped the political responses of the nationalist community. As with Unionists, there are extreme and moderate positions. Sinn Fein and the Irish Republican Army (IRA) represent the extreme view, supporting violence as a legitimate tactic and finding expression in the various campaigns of the IRA. This approach is strongly opposed by the moderate nationalist position, represented by the Social Democratic and Labour Party (SDLP).

(A) Sinn Fein and the Irish Republican Army (IRA)

The Provisional IRA grew out of the current violence. There had been an IRA in existence since the 1920s, committed to the violent overthrow of the Northern state and the removal of the British from Ireland. As discussed in Chapter 3, by the 1950s this organisation had lost the support of most Nationalists in Northern Ireland. Republican extremism was seen by them as an irrelevance.

By way of a response, the IRA decided to take a more political approach. Dominated, at that time, by left-wingers from the Republic of Ireland, they adopted a marxist political ideology, which to many traditional Republicans sat uneasily with their Catholicism, and they decided to eschew violence. As Bishop and Mallie (1987) argue, the IRA had moved to a position such that by 1968 they had little in the way of weapons. Indeed, during the loyalist attacks on the Catholic ghettos in August 1969, they were seen by many residents as not defending their areas. As already recorded in Chapter 4, graffiti in Catholic areas declared that 'IRA = I ran away' (Arthur and Jeffrey 1988, p. 37).

As a result of this violence the more conservative elements within the IRA decided to rearm. A split took place within the movement, between those who accepted the new doctrine of marxist-inspired politics and the more traditional republicans. The former became known as the Official IRA. While they too engaged in acts of violence, eventually they declared a ceasefire and created a new political party, the Workers' Party, which is strongly anti-terrorist in philosophy, as well as being left-wing. Indeed, the Workers' Party, while attracting most of its fairly limited number of votes (about 1 to 3 per cent of those voting) from among the nationalist community, is perhaps the nationalist party closest to unionist thinking. For example, it has argued for a devolved Parliament and Government, but without the need for a power-sharing arrangement. The Workers' Party has made some strides in the Republic of Ireland, securing some seats in the Dail (Parliament). Recently it has argued the case for extradition of suspected terrorists from the Republic to Northern Ireland. The party has therefore developed in a quite radical direction since the early 1970s.

The members of the IRA who rejected the leadership broke away to form the Provisionals (or PIRA as they are frequently known). They were born out of the Catholic ghettos. While having links with southern Republicans, PIRA is essentially a northern organisation, increasingly dominated by those from the republican enclaves in Northern Ireland. There can be little doubt about the ruthlessness of the organisation, nor about its ability to sustain a long campaign.

Up until quite recently the weapons PIRA used were military and propaganda, the latter particularly in the USA. A new strategy has emerged, summed up in the phrase used by Danny Morrison, Sinn Fein Director of Publicity, at their annual conference in 1981, 'a ballot paper in one hand and an Armalite rifle in the other'. In other words, in addition to the violence, the Provisionals see advantages in developing a political approach. Hence Sinn Fein, which is the political party identified with PIRA, contests elections to local councils, Westminster and the European Parliament.

This represents a major change in tactics for PIRA, since in the past it has taken the view that even to contest an election to any of the governmental institutions in either part of Ireland was to confer a legitimacy on them to which they were not entitled. The tactic has had some success. First, Gerry Adams was elected MP for West Belfast. The important point was that this demonstrated that PIRA had a significant measure of support among Catholics. Second, a number of candidates – 59 in the 1985 local government elections – were successful in securing election to various local councils. As a result the government was embarrassed and unionist disenchantment increased. Unionists fail to understand why they should be expected to work with Sinn Fein councillors, some of whom have been in prison for various terrorist offences. These feelings are increased as some Unionist councillors are targets for PIRA attack.

The new tactic also led to meetings between the leaders of

Sinn Fein and the SDLP: a sign perhaps that the political approach made Republicanism slightly more respectable. Nothing came of these meetings – except the possibility that dialogue within Northern Ireland between the SDLP and Unionists was made more difficult. But they were a sign that some Sinn Fein members recognised that violence by itself was unlikely to achieve their objectives.

It should be said nevertheless that 'the Armalite and the ballot' approach has some drawbacks for the Republicans. First, there is the possibility that it will generate some tension between the politicians and the military men. This has emerged in a number of ways, with prominent Sinn Fein spokespersons being forced to condemn a number of PIRA atrocities. In the long term this might lead to a weakening of PIRA. Second, it has also led to a split within PIRA, with an older, more traditional, group of Republicans creating a new party.

Third, while the election results demonstrate that Sinn Fein and PIRA have some support, they also make perfectly clear that their views are minority ones. Even among the Catholic population in Northern Ireland they have no more than the support of about one third. Their support in elections in the Republic of Ireland show them to be a marginal party. Unlike the Workers' Party, Sinn Fein has no MPs in the Dail and seems unlikely to secure any seats in the near future. Clearly any claim from the Provisionals that they represent the people of Ireland, or even the Catholic people in the north, has no basis in fact.

(B) The Social Democratic and Labour Party (SDLP)

The more moderate nationalist position is represented by the Social Democratic and Labour Party (SDLP). The SDLP was founded in 1970, with support drawn from among various nationally-oriented opposition MPs at Stormont, including John Hume and Gerry Fitt, its first leader. It is the main political party in the minority community and has been the most successful to come from that community since the origins of the state.

The old Nationalist Party (see McAllister 1983, pp. 71–3) in many senses was not a political party at all. For most of its history it was not organised and did not have a set of policies beyond incantations about the dismantling of Northern Ireland. It is, of course, true that there was little incentive for it to act as a normal political party. Its role was as a permanent opposition. Up to its demise in the late 1960s, it had managed to have passed one single piece of legislation, namely the Wild Birds Act 1931.

The title of the SDLP indicates that it sees itself as a socialist party, and indeed it is a member of the Socialist International. But its social and economic policies are not especially socialist, and they indicate that it is a moderate, left-of-centre party. The other dimension of the SDLP is that it is a nationalist party, believing in the eventual unification of Ireland. *But*, the SDLP argues that this can only be brought about through consent – through some sort of political or constitutional action.

While non-violence has been central to the SDLP's approach, it has, on occasions, adopted extra-constitutional action as a tactic. This includes withdrawing from formal political processes. For example, between July 1971 and March 1972, the various nationalist political parties withdrew from Stormont and, after the introduction of internment in August 1972, SDLP councillors withdrew from local authorities.

The combined effects of the collapse of the Power-Sharing Executive and the rise of Sinn Fein as an electoral force have had a profound effect on the SDLP. The Party has increasingly argued that a solution to the problems of Northern Ireland cannot be found if an all-Ireland dimension is excluded. There have been signs that this view has found increasing favour within the Party. For example, having participated in the Power-Sharing Executive in 1972, ten years later it boycotted the Assembly.

Its developing concern with Irish nationalism led to the establishment of the New Ireland Forum, the purpose of which was to redefine Irish nationalism in the light of contemporary events and attitudes. The Forum involved the SDLP and the three main parties in the Republic. Its *Report*, published in May 1984, put forward a number of models through which Irish unity could be achieved. But it emphasised that such unity could only be achieved through consent.

The Forum *Report* was one of the contributory factors to the creation in 1985 of the Anglo-Irish Agreement, which was received by the SDLP as a vindication of their position. John Hume, leader of the SDLP, is widely regarded as one of the leading architects of the Agreement. The Party took credit among the nationalist community for its signing and used it in its competition with Sinn Fein for the nationalist vote. While there have been complaints among SDLP members that it has not led to all the changes that they anticipated, by and large they are still the strongest supporters of the pact.

Conclusion: intra-communal party competition

These, then, are the main party-political actors within Northern Ireland. The principal changes that have occurred in the last twenty years have been first the break-up of the Unionist Party, a break-up that has stabilised around three parties, a moderate Alliance Party, and the OUP and DUP; and second the emergence of two organised nationalist/republican parties.

Essentially, party competition has been intra-communal, with the OUP and DUP fighting for the unionist vote and the SDLP and Sinn Fein for votes among the minority community. The Alliance Party, and other bi-confessional parties, are still relatively marginalised, although assisted by the proportional representation system of voting that is used in Northern Ireland for local government European elections and such other elections as are held, apart from those for Westminster.

It is unlikely that this party structure will alter in the foreseeable future. The present parties seem likely to continue to be the principal political actors, and the next chapter examines their impact on the policy-making process.

7

Policy-making in Northern Ireland

This chapter examines how policies, particularly in fields such as education, health and industrial development, are made for Northern Ireland. An important issue is the extent to which policies on these subjects are different in Northern Ireland from what they are in other parts of the United Kingdom.

Pressure for common standards

While the immediate reaction of many to this question is to declare 'of course Northern Ireland is different', a number of influential commentators have argued that most policies in each of the four countries of the United Kingdom are basically similar in aim and content, despite different arrangements for their administration.

For example, Richard Rose (1982, p. 111) has argued that the majority of policies adopted in the United Kingdom are what he terms *concurrent policies*, that is 'programmes with the same function throughout the United Kingdom but delivered by different institutions in different parts'. He goes on to declare that 'concurrent policies are meant to be harmonious, that is, consistent with each other except for administrative differentiation' (Rose 1982, p. 112). Rose therefore would anticipate that most policies in Northern Ireland – there are obvious exceptions in the field of law and order – would be broadly similar to those in other parts of the United Kingdom.

A variety of reasons have been advanced to support this view. These include the propositions that people throughout the United Kingdom demand the same level of service provision and that the dominant professional bodies and pressure groups, which are organised nationally, operate within a broad view of what is acceptable practice in their field and bring pressure to ensure common standards throughout the United Kingdom.

This chapter explores some of these issues. The next section discusses some of the elements that might constitute a Northern Ireland policy community. This is followed by an analysis of how that community deals with the particular politics of Northern Ireland. Finally, the issue of the degree of autonomy of the regional policy community from Whitehall is explored.

The Northern Ireland policy community

Rod Rhodes (1985, 1988) has articulated the concept of *policy networks* as a way of understanding the policy process in the United Kingdom. Such networks are defined as a 'complex of organisations connected to each other by resource dependencies and distinguished from other . . . complexes by breaks in the structure of resource dependencies' (Benson 1982, p. 148). Rhodes argues that there are a number of different types of networks that can be distinguished. Among them are what he calls 'territorial policy communities' (Rhodes 1988, p. 78). Their characteristics include stability of relationships, continuity of a highly restrictive membership, vertical interdependence based on shared delivery responsibilities and insulation from other networks and, invariably, from the general public (including Parliament). They have a high degree of vertical interdependence and limited horizontal articulation. They are also highly integrated.

Policy-making in Scotland, Wales and Northern Ireland is generated by networks with the above characteristics, according to Rhodes. Such networks are concerned to defend their territorial interests as best they can. Whether they succeed in the sense that they develop policy initiatives relevant to their region's society or are dominated by Whitehall is a question that will be considered in more detail at a later stage. At this point, it is worth describing some of the main actors in this tight, integrated community.

A number of authorities (Saunders 1983) have argued that policy-making at the regional level is dominated by bureaucratic and professional interests. In other words, it is to be expected that the civil service, particularly in view of the structure of government, would play a key role in policy-making in Northern Ireland. But other actors who are liable to be involved are politicians, other public officials, trade unions, employers' organisations and pressure groups. The previous chapters describe the principal features of various public sector organisations, and the main political parties. There have not been many studies of the impact of pressure groups on policy in Northern Ireland (see Birrell and Murie 1980, chapter six). The influence of the Orange Order on a number of policies, and the role of the churches on education policy, are perhaps the most obvious exceptions. In addition, the trade unions and employer organisations are usually considered two important influences on public policy developments. It is useful at this stage to describe aspects of the structure and role of these four organisations.

(A) The Orange Order

The origins of the Orange Order are to be found in the sectarian violence of the eighteenth century, as outlined in Chapter Two. The fortunes of the Order declined during the nineteenth century, only to be revived during the Home Rule crises of the late nineteenth and early twentieth centuries. The Order's official view of itself is a religious organisation. In practice its central objectives are a mixture of the religious and political, defending the Protestant religion and supporting the maintenance of the Union with Britain. For many years the Order had close links with the Unionist Party. It was represented on the Party's Central Council (Harbinson 1973). Traditionally, members of the Unionist Party who aspired to become MPs were members of the Order, though there were occasional exceptions.

The Order played a significant part in uniting Unionists, particularly during the first fifty years of the existence of the Northern Ireland state. Lyons (1973, p. 720) indicates that during this period some two-thirds of the adult male Protestant population belonged to the Order and that it performed two important functions. First, with its public displays of ceremony it provided the Ulster Unionist with 'much of the colour and drama of his creed' (Lyons 1973, p. 720). Second, it served as a link between different sections of Protestant society. During the 1970s and 1980s, when Stormont no longer existed and there was considerable political tension among Unionists as to the way forward, the Order declined in importance. It still retains close links with the Official Unionist Party (OUP), and many Unionist politicians still pay homage to it. But it does not have the influence on government that it once had.

This influence was seen at its most public over various attempts, particularly before the Second World War, to reform the education system in Northern Ireland. It has also expressed views on moral issues, for example proposals to change legislation on homosexuality and licensing. In general, when the Order had a clear view on a particular policy, during the existence of Stormont, it was able to ensure that this was implemented.

(B) The churches

In Northern Ireland a higher percentage of the population declare an adherence to religion than in any other part of the United Kingdom. One might, then, expect that the role of the churches concerning certain issues would be significant, and indeed on issues such as education and moral matters they have played an important role.

For example, both Protestant and Catholic churches reacted with considerable opposition to the proposals contained in Lord Londonderry's Education Act 1923, described in Chapter 3. The Protestant churches formed a pressure group, the United Education Committee of the Protestant Churches, to co-ordinate the campaign in conjunction with the Orange Order against the legislation. The Committee had a considerable measure of success in securing the changes it wanted and was brought into action again during the 1940s when further legislative proposals in education were seen by the Protestant churches as threatening.

The Roman Catholic Church has also sought to preserve and protect its interests in education matters, though not quite with the same measure of success as its Protestant counterparts. This was a reflection of the wider political positions in Northern Ireland. Over time, however, the Catholic Church secured a considerable number of its demands for increased support for its schools. More recently, its opposition to the various proposals to reform teacher training by, *inter alia*, locating teacher training colleges on one site, was successful in securing the defeat of this measure.

(C) Trade unions

The organisation of the trade-union movement in Northern Ireland is complex. There are unions which are all-Ireland based, for example, the Irish Teachers National Organisation; there are also unions which are centred on Northern Ireland, for example the Ulster Teachers Union; however, the vast majority of unions are United Kingdom based, though organised regionally, for example the National Union of Teachers (Blease 1984).

The main central body is the Northern Ireland Committee of the Irish Committee of Trade Unions (NIC–ICTU). ICTU is an all-Ireland organisation, a fact which prevented it from being recognised and consulted by the Stormont government for many years. This was achieved finally when Terence O'Neill wished to set up an economic council, modelled on the National Economic Development Office. The trade unions were not prepared to co-operate without being recognised. ICTU changed aspects of its constitution at that time in order to devolve certain functions on to NIC-ICTU. As a result the Northern Ireland government granted recognition.

Since then, NIC-ICTU has been involved on a number of

statutory bodies, including the Northern Ireland Economic Council and the Northern Ireland Training Council. The unions' influence varies with the issue and with the attitude of the government in power. Currently, as in other parts of the United Kingdom, their influence has waned.

NIC-ICTU has had an important role in keeping sectarianism out of the workplace. In addition, NIC-ICTU's influence on ICTU generally is important. The Irish trade-union movement has roots in republicanism, but NIC-ICTU ensures that expressions of republicanism are to some degree limited. Both of these aspects of NIC-ICTU's activities afford the trade-union movement a degree of influence in Northern Ireland that it might not otherwise have.

NIC-ICTU also consults on a formal basis with the UK Trades Union Congress (TUC). According to Blease (1984, p. 20), these consultations take place over issues such as industrial legislation and social and economic matters which affect Northern Ireland workers but are under the direct influence of mainland departments.

(D) Employers

The main employers' organisation is the regional organisation of the Confederation of British Industry (CBI-NI) though there are also organisations such as the Institute of Directors. With respect to CBI-NI, policy is largely dictated by London, though the regional organisation is not without influence on Northern Ireland issues. In general, however, the CBI-NI is probably less autonomous than the NIC-ICTU.

Like its trade-union counterpart, CBI-NI is the main channel through which employers are represented on a number of public agencies in Northern Ireland. On the whole, the employers have had less difficulty in securing entry into the policy process than the unions. That is a reflection of the fact that the employers had a strong base in the Unionist Party. In addition, in an economically-deprived region such as Northern Ireland, it was important to listen to the concerns of employers if employment was to be protected.

The policy community at work

Turning to consider how the Northern Ireland policy community operates, and the extent to which it is autonomous from policy-making at the UK national level, the first point to note is that it operates differently depending on the *nature* and *type* of policy issue. Three broad types of issues can be distinguished:

1. The Northern Ireland problem.
2. Finance and public expenditure.
3. Other issues of policy.

On the first type of issue the Northern Ireland Office (NIO) takes the lead; the Department of Finance and Personnel (DFP) in conjunction with NIO is the crucial focus for the second group of issues; and a complex series of relationships are involved in the last group, but with the Northern Ireland Departments (NIDs) playing a crucial role.

Issues around the Northern Ireland problem

The first group of policy issues concern the interconnected problems related to the constitutional and security position of Northern Ireland. These include the continuing search to find a set of acceptable governmental structures and the development of appropriate security policies.

In these matters, the Secretary of State is a key figure, along with senior civil servants, particularly those from NIO. But there are a number of other important factors. Given the international interest that the Northern Ireland problem generates – it appears, for example, that European and United States influences were important in developing the Anglo-Irish Agreement – it is not surprising to find that the Foreign Office has an interest in Northern Ireland matters. Obviously the other major interested department is the Ministry of Defence. A substantial number of military personnel are deployed in the territory, and clearly major policy initiatives require the involvement of this Department.

These issues affect the whole of Northern Ireland and are fundamental to its politics. Not surprisingly, its politicians and people have a major interest in the outcome and must, at the end of the day, determine the nature of the solution – if solution there is to be. There are also pressure groups of various kinds which have come into existence to try to influence these matters. Some of these have played a significant part in various ways: for example the Northern Ireland Civil Rights Association. In addition, a number of the more established groups have expressed views on various aspects of the problem. For example, the churches have been active in attempting to resolve the problem.

The next chapter considers this policy field in further detail. It is clearly the most important of the policy concerns affecting Northern Ireland, as well as the most complex. The policy network is at its most fractured and involves a wide number of actors and potential actors. Attempting to manage such a network is very difficult.

Finance and public expenditure issues

The concept of a closed, integrated policy community has most relevance in the field of finance and public expenditure matters. The key relationship is that of the Department of Finance and Personnel (DFP) and the UK Treasury, a relationship widely described in terms of mutual trust and understanding. The essentials of the current process for determining the total and distribution of public expenditure in Northern Ireland were first articulated in a 1974 paper *Finance and the Economy*, and remain broadly the same. The underlying principle is encapsulated in the term 'parity', which the discussion paper accepts is a 'convenient shorthand for a very complex arrangement' (p. 16). The basic definition, which was formally agreed between the Northern Ireland and United Kingdom governments in 1938, was that 'any deficit on the Northern Ireland budget which was neither the result of a standard of social expenditure higher than, nor of taxation lower than, that of Great Britain would be made good by the United Kingdom Government' (*Finance and the Economy* (1974), p. 16).

While parity is easy to determine in respect of certain services, for example cash social security benefits, a variety of methods have been required to ensure that it is achieved for other services. 'In practice the implementation of the parity principle depends on individual judgments and decisions with consultation between . . . [the Department of Finance and Personnel (DFP)] and the Treasury as necessary' (*Finance and the Economy* (1974), p. 16). The situation grew even more complex when the principle was extended to enable Northern Ireland to catch up to Great Britain's standards in certain services and to offset the economic disadvantages arising from Northern Ireland's geographical isolation.

The public expenditure total

Ministers consistently point out that Northern Ireland is treated more generously than other parts of the United Kingdom. They justify this by reference to the economic and social problems in Northern Ireland. The government has been subject to criticisms from some of its own back-benchers over what they regard as a too-generous allocation. See, for example, the statement in the House of Commons by Michael Fallon, MP for Darlington (Appropriation (Northern Ireland) Debate, *House of Commons Official Debates*, 24 Feburary 1987, cols. 237–8). On the other hand, the argument has been put that current levels of public expenditure are 'clearly inadequate to provide parity with the economic conditions experienced in the United Kingdom as a whole' (Northern Ireland Economic Council, *Report No. 42*, 1984).

It was only in the 1970s that public expenditure per head in Northern Ireland drew level with other parts of the United Kingdom. In 1962–3, Northern Ireland's identifiable public expenditure per head was 8 per cent lower than England's, 7 per cent less than Wales' and 24 per cent less than Scotland's (*Needs Assessment Study* 1979). By 1977–8, Northern Ireland's position had become much more favourable, and the comparable figure is 41 per cent *above* both England and Wales, and 13 per cent above Scotland.

The Northern Ireland Economic Council, in its 1986–7 *Annual Report*, argues that although the gross differential in public expenditure per head between Northern Ireland and Great Britain had increased from 30.5 per cent in 1980–1 to 39.3 per cent in 1985–6, this later figure declines to 5.4 per cent when factors such as migration, the impact of national policies and different administrative arrangements are taken into account. It concludes that this is not excessive, given 'our major economic difficulties' (Northern Ireland Economic Council, *Report No. 67*, 1987). Simple per capita comparisons are misleading in that they do not take account of the relative neglect of the past, as well as different needs.

In deciding on the total public expenditure for Northern Ireland, DFP and the Treasury, in the first instance, negotiate over the total public expenditure allocation. The parity principle enters into the negotiations in that it contributes to building up the elements that go to make the total. The Secretary of State may be required to intervene with the Chief Secretary of the Treasury if the discussions between officials run into difficulties.

The pattern of public expenditure

Once the total is decided, it is then up to the Secretary of State, after receiving appropriate advice, to allocate the monies between the various demands in the light of his priorities and subject to the various constraints. According to the 1987 *Public Expenditure White Paper* there are four categories of expenditure within the responsibility of the Secretary of State. These are:

1. Law, order, protective and other services by NIO.
2. Social security benefits.
3. Certain national agricultural support schemes which are now transferred to the Department of Agriculture for Northern Ireland (DANI).
4. Other expenditure by the Northern Ireland Departments (NIDs), area boards, district councils and other agencies and institutions.

Provision for social security is determined by the number of beneficiaries within national policy and cannot be altered by the Secretary of State for Northern Ireland. The European Community, as well as the national government, has a considerable influence in determining category (3), and monies within this category are not transferable.

The Secretary of State can decide on the allocation among categories (1) and (4). However, in practice, the scope for flexibility is limited. For example, public sector pay settlements are largely determined in the United Kingdom as a whole. In addition, large programmes acquire a momentum of their own and are difficult to change within the survey period (Quigley 1987, p. 292).

The Treasury does not become involved in discussions associated with categories (1) and (4) unless decisions have implications for the rest of the United Kingdom. For example, before its privatisation subsidies to the shipbuilders Harland and Wolff could be cited as precedent by other yards in Britain. Hence Her Majesty's Treasury (HMT) would wish to assure itself that it could live with the implications.

With respect to categories (1) and (4), the priority spending areas have been law and order and industrial development. Until 1987, housing was accorded a high priority. The first two are perhaps obvious, but the third policy area is interesting in the light of national policy developments. This is examined later in this chapter.

To sum up, the finance and public expenditure policy issues are dealt with through a series of negotiations with a relatively few influential actors. It is a comparatively closed network, with much trust and goodwill between the main actors.

Other policy issues

Finally, there are the remaining policy areas which include education, health and housing. In each case the central institution is the appropriate Northern Ireland department, with a variety of other organisations, including quangos and interested groups, as well as Whitehall departments and, on occasions, other NIDs, involved.

The particular configuration will depend on the area and the issue. However, the relationship between the Northern Ireland department and its Whitehall counterpart is important. Policies emanating from the Whitehall department are given serious consideration, it being recognised that the Whitehall department will often have more individuals to deploy on research into an issue and are liable to reflect government thinking on particular topics. Nevertheless, it is also true that Whitehall departments do not usually have the same interest in what happens in Northern Ireland. This results in a measure of autonomy in policy-making for Northern Ireland policymakers.

One important factor that influences policy developments is the political divisions within Northern Ireland. Education is a good example of a policy area which has been shaped in part by the political and religious divisions. The educational system reflects the sectarian divide, with Roman Catholic and Protestant children for the most part being taught separately (Akenson 1973; Osbourne *et al.* 1987).

The importance of this for policy developments can be illustrated in a number of incidents. For example, in June 1977 the Labour Government declared its intention of abolishing the selection system at 11 – still maintained in Northern Ireland – and restructuring the educational system, moving away from the dominance of the grammar schools in secondary education. A considerable amount of resistance to this developed and this initiative fell with the defeat of the Labour Government in 1979.

One of the elements in the equation which contributed to the policy being stalled was the role of the voluntary grammar schools – which represent the majority of grammar schools in the province. These are church-owned, and to remove them would have had implications for Church–State relations. In short, the structure of the Northern Ireland education system owes a great deal to the nature of Northern Ireland society.

The autonomy of the policy process

This is one example of the way in which policy in Northern Ireland has to take account of the peculiar political circumstances of Northern Ireland, but even within education there are many examples in which Northern Ireland has adopted

Whitehall initiatives. The existence of the grammar schools and the eleven-plus owes a great deal to policies that emanated in Whitehall. The question remains concerning the extent to which the Northern Ireland policy network is able to act autonomously from Whitehall in determining policies for Northern Ireland.

This can be considered in two stages. Prior to Direct Rule, there is evidence which suggests that the devolved government had a reasonable degree of autonomy, though constrained by financial and political considerations. While the concept of parity was important, especially in financial terms, and thus represented a very real constraint upon the Northern Ireland government, there is clear evidence that 'Northern Ireland and its government could, and did, diverge substantially from the standards and legislation operating in Great Britain and at Westminster' (Birrell and Murie 1980, p. 266).

The extent to which the Stormont government developed a policy direction independent of Westminster in the areas for which it was charged with responsibility depended upon a variety of factors, including the degree of political passion the policy issue aroused in Northern Ireland and the necessity of securing finance from Westminster. As already described, education is a good example of the former. Social security payments represent an example of an issue where monies had to be obtained from Westminster. As this was the key factor, rates of payment introduced in Northern Ireland were identical to those in the rest of the United Kingdom.

Since Direct Rule the pressure for uniformity with Westminster has increased for a variety of reasons. Birrell and Murie (1980) argue that Stormont discretion operated to some extent because of the absence of Westminster pressure. That is no longer true. Northern Ireland matters are raised in the House of Commons. Westminster politicians are likely to be more aware of Northern Ireland practice and to examine policy proposals in the light of their own experience. Thus, for example, ministers know that much more is being spent per head in Northern Ireland on the health service than in their own constituencies in the rest of the United Kingdom.

It is undeniable that, since Direct Rule, policy-making within Northern Ireland has come much more within the overall thrust of British policies, with variations occurring in the implementation and administration rather than in the central direction of the policy. However, that is not a guarantee that every British policy initiative will be duplicated in Northern Ireland. The extent to which Northern Ireland practice will differ from that adopted in the rest of the United Kingdom will depend partly on the different administrative arrangements, partly on the political sensitivity of an issue and partly on the perceived need within Northern Ireland.

The housing policy network

In order to see how policy emerges and is affected by both regional and national influences it is useful to examine a policy area in some depth. The field of housing provides a good opportunity to see a policy network in operation.

A considerable number of institutions are involved in the housing policy network, including public and private organisations. It has even been suggested that the security services have an input (Cowan 1982; Singleton 1985). Some of the organisations are purely regional institutions, while others are regional branches of national bodies.

Building societies, various professional bodies and the construction industry all play a part in housing policy development, but their desire and ability to influence housing policy directly at regional level varies. For example, the construction industry in Northern Ireland is organised regionally, though with national contacts, and its representative organisation – The Federation of Building and Civil Engineering Contractors (Northern Ireland) Ltd – is in constant contact with relevant regional government agencies.

This mode of organisation is not surprising given that the construction industry is a key element in the economy, with many small firms heavily dependent on housing expenditure. While there is a regional organisation of building societies in Northern Ireland – the Association of Building Societies – they generally would see their influence operating principally at national level. In addition, and centrally, there are the public organisations such as the Northern Ireland Housing Executive

(NIHE), the Northern Ireland Department of the Environment
(DOE[NI]) and local government.

The structure of this network owes a great deal to the social
and economic environment in which it is embedded. Two features, which have already been alluded to, are particularly
important: the poor quality of housing and the sectarianism of
Northern Ireland's politics.

The poor quality of the housing stock is discussed in
Chapter 1. In addition, housing policy has been made more
complicated by the sectarian nature of political and social life
in Northern Ireland. Poole (1982) has stated that in a number
of towns and cities there is a considerable degree of religious
segregation. Both communities are intensely aware of territory,
both their own and that of the other community. Consequently,
housing estates in many towns tend to reflect this sectarian
division (Singleton 1982b and 1985).

Negotiation and Accommodation

At the regional level, housing policy emerges from negotiation
and discussion between the Executive and Department of the
Environment (NI). The simplistic but erroneous view is that
the Department is responsible for policy-formulation and the
Executive for service-delivery. This view ignores two complicating factors. First, on questions of housing, the Department and
the Minister operate in a sensitive political arena and matters
of detail easily become highly contentious.

Second, within the Executive there is the strongly held view
that, as a considerable amount of housing expertise lies within
the organisation, it should contribute to the development of
policies in housing. Staff in the Executive constantly argue that
they are in a 'comprehensive housing agency' with a responsibility for housing throughout Northern Ireland. The result is
that a clear role definition is difficult, with much negotiation
and interplay taking place between the two organisations.

While the literature on inter-governmental relationships
reminds us that such exchanges involve more than the constitutional and legal dimensions (Rhodes 1981, 1985), it is clear,
as already described, that these are weighted in favour of the
DOE(NI). However the Executive has considerable housing

expertise, is largely relative to the Department's housing section and is the principal deliverer of public housing services. Further, many Board members, while formally appointed by the Minister, owe their appointment to political considerations over which he has little control. This affords them greater autonomy than might otherwise be the case. Complicating the issue further is the fact that DOE(NI) is responsible for a range of other key environmental services, including planning and roads. Hence the pattern of interrelationships between NIHE and DOE(NI) can be quite complex.

Finally, councillors have a measure of influence on the housing policy decisions, and some councillors are well placed to exert considerable influence, through for example the Housing Council. Council members bring to bear on the policy process their rights of access as provided by the legislation and their resources as elected councillors. Councillors can generate political interest in issues and Executive officers do not relish unnecessary conflicts with councillors.

The skills of councillors at employing these resources appear to be a significant factor in determining the degree of influence they achieve. One important dimension which a number of them suggested was vital was the style of approach.

Within the Executive it is felt that many Council members are overly interested in details and in making 'irresponsible' statements. Executive personnel on the whole are critical of councillors' contributions to the policy debate. NIHE officers recognise that councillors are public representatives with a legitimate interest in the concerns of their constituents and access to the media, which might be helpful to NIHE on occasions. In general, local authorities, though having more influence than they are willing to admit, are much less influential than elsewhere in the United Kingdom.

A measure of autonomy

Clearly, one would expect to find some tensions existing in the network. Some of these are due to differing political ideologies. And there have been other tensions (though not of the same degree) about appropriate roles and relationships, for example between the Department and the Executive and, within the

Executive, between regions and the centre. In addition the three central actors (Executive, Department and local government) interact with the other organisations in the network in varying ways. For example, private-sector contractors rely on NIHE for a great deal of business. They would not have the same relationship with either DOE or local authorities.

Despite these conflicts, it is clear that the network has a high degree of stability and coherence. This is due, in part, to the dominance of the NIHE and DOE(NI). The size of Northern Ireland means that key decision-makers generally know each other. It is hence easy for information about issues to pass around and this tends to cement the network.

There has been a tradition that housing is a policy issue concerning which decisions are taken at regional level. This is partly because it was one of the matters for the devolved Parliament and one on which that Parliament was prepared to take a line different from that taken by the rest of the United Kingdom (Birrell and Murie 1980). While policies in Northern Ireland are in general closer to those in Britain since Direct Rule, Northern Ireland civil servants are quite clear that housing remains a regional matter under the current constitutional arrangements.

There is some evidence that housing policy has developed in ways that provide some interesting contrasts with the rest of the United Kingdom and suggest that, while conscious of Whitehall pressures, the network operates with a measure of autonomy. Housing is a policy issue on which the Thatcher government had – and continues to have – a very definite policy stance. As Malpass and Murie (1982, p. 55) argue:

> The policies of the Thatcher Government, carried through in the 1980 Housing Act, represent a clear break with the past and a marked shift to the right. No previous government has been so determined, nor gone so far, to reduce public expenditure on housing, to reduce the size and role of the public sector, and to restrict the autonomy of local authorities in matters of housing policy.

These general policy objectives have manifested themselves in specific programmes such as a reduction in public expenditure on housing and in public-sector new builds, an increase in public-sector rents and the expansion of the right to buy public-sector houses. In turn this has meant an expansion in private-sector housing and an increase in home ownership. Murie (1985) has argued that, by and large, the government has been successful in implementing these policies nationally.

Pull towards Whitehall

Given the clear and definite policy stance of the government, one would expect to see its approach applied in Northern Ireland as elsewhere in the United Kingdom. On the other hand, the unique features of housing in Northern Ireland suggest that if the regional policy network wished to resist its implementation these might enable it to be successful.

In 1981 the Secretary of State declared housing as a priority, with the result that public expenditure on housing in Northern Ireland has represented a higher proportionate share of public expenditure resources than elsewhere in the United Kingdom, reflecting Northern Ireland's greater housing needs and the government's continuing commitment to the housing programme. Between 1980–1 and 1985–6 there was an increase of 67 per cent in cash terms and about 22 per cent in real terms in gross expenditure on housing (*Government's Expenditure Plans* 1987). This was due in part to the ability of the Executive to provide evidence about the poor quality of housing in Northern Ireland. NIHE also helped to finance the increase in public housing by its ability to generate funds partly because of a successful house sales policy. In addition, councillors and other influential parties lobbied a broadly sympathetic Secretary of State, James Prior. The result was an increase in public expenditure on housing.

In 1987, the Secretary of State indicated that housing would no longer receive such favoured treatment. The net cash allocation on the housing programme was planned to fall from £340 million in 1988–9 to £330 million in 1989–90 and again to £320 million in 1990–1. This represents a substantial decline if a direct comparison is made with the 1987 White Paper, where the 1988–9 and 1989–90 figures were £370 million and £380 million respectively.

The reasons offered for this change in priority status of housing include some success in improving housing standards in Northern Ireland and growing pressures from other programmes. However, the Government claims that public expenditure on housing in Northern Ireland is still continuing at a level well in excess of the level per head of population in Britain.

What can be learned from this case study about policy-making in Northern Ireland? Policies do not occur in a vacuum. They have to take account of the social, economic and political constraints. It is obvious therefore that there is a degree of autonomy in policy matters. But there are limits. Over time, there is a pull towards adopting Whitehall policies, particularly where there is a government as committed to a certain policy perspective as the current one.

During the last ten years, government policies for Northern Ireland, particularly in areas such as health, education and housing, increasingly reflect what is happening in the rest of the United Kingdom. Thus, health policies as defined in the White Paper *Working for Patients* are being applied in Northern Ireland. Equally, the Government's education policies, as embodied in the 1988 Education Reform Act, are central to the Education Reform (Northern Ireland) Order 1989. There are differences in each case. For example, the latter has some concerns with integrated education that is reflective of the particular concerns of Northern Ireland. But the central ideas are rooted in policies already articulated at Westminster.

Policy implementation: the delivery of services

There is another dimension to policy-making, namely implementation. Policies may be announced, but if they are not carried through, they have little or no impact on the lives of those they are supposed to affect. For example, privatisation, in all its guises, has been central to the approach of Thatcher Government. In Northern Ireland, while there were various statements about privatisation, in fact it was only from 1988–9 that serious efforts were made to implement it.

Policy implementation is about how services are delivered.

There is strong evidence that the sectarian division has had a considerable impact on the local delivery of services. For example, in housing many towns have a clear division between Catholic and Protestant housing estates. This has been reinforced recently with intimidation growing due to the increased tension generated by the Anglo-Irish Agreement. As a result, there has been some population movement, though not as significant as occurred in the late 1960s and early 1970s.

A number of problems have been presented to the Housing Executive as a result. First, the NIHE has had to respond to the immediate problem caused by intimidation by providing emergency housing. Second, the Executive is constrained in any attempts to provide integrated housing. Indeed, in Belfast, in conjunction with DOE(NI) it has had to erect walls designed to separate the communities. Third, NIHE has had to take into account the fact that the building trades have traditionally been divided along sectarian lines. This can affect building programmes in various ways.

The example of NIHE is but one case in which in the Northern Ireland situation public-sector organisations are under scrutiny by both sides of the community. One important aspect of this is their employment practices. Here the work of the Fair Employment Agency (FEA) is important. The FEA has conducted investigations into a number of public-sector organisations including the civil service, the Housing Executive, universities, area boards and some local authorities.

With respect to the civil service, FEA concluded that prior to 1970 the number of Roman Catholics in the Northern Ireland Civil Service was 'very low' in comparison to their proportion in the total population. The FEA reported that the position had greatly improved through the 1970s. In general the civil service are more aware of the importance of recruiting across the community. A unit has been formed with responsibility for monitoring employment. Certain difficulties still remain, particularly in respect of the number of Catholics at senior levels. But there is little doubt that NICS has a highly sophisticated monitoring system and is most anxious to remove any barriers to fair employment opportunities (Osbourne and Cormack 1989).

The records of other public organisations vary. The 1985

FEA report on the Housing Executive concluded that the organisation was providing equal opportunities for both sections of the community. The major area of continuing difficulty with respect to employment practices is in the local authorities, a number of which resent the activities of the FEA. But even here recruitment procedures are now much more bureaucratised and officials, at least, are sensitive to the implications of the FEA and recommendations emanating from it.

Relations between politicians and officials

This leads on to the question of the relationships between politicians and officials. It would appear that officials resist any attempt to draw them into what they perceive as sectarian politics. But they have considerable sensitivity for the community implications of policy decisions. Indeed, given the absence of public agencies under local political control, public administrators, particularly the civil service, have assumed considerable influence. As a former head of the Northern Ireland Civil Service said:

> . . . one of the interesting consequences of direct rule was that many senior members of the NICS found themselves more closely involved with political affairs than before. . . . Previously many of the senior members of the NICS felt that as members of the divided community in which they lived they had to avoid expressing views on sensitive political questions. . . . Now civil servants found themselves obliged to bring all their local knowledge fully to bear on the decision-making process and having to accept the risk that if they were thought to be actively involved in giving advice on political aspects of their work their impartiality as members of the NICS might be jeopardised. (Bell 1985, p. 12)

Clearly in this position it is important that public bureaucracies are seen to be neutral. This is a remarkably difficult task to achieve. The civil service, despite the problems mentioned earlier, has probably come closest. This may well be because it does not deliver controversial services, particularly housing.

The conclusions that can be drawn from the Northern Ireland experience have to be tempered with the awareness of the nature of the conflict. Returning to the description, outlined earlier, of politics in Northern Ireland, two elements help in understanding the role of the public bureaucracies. One is that the Northern Ireland public administration system is rooted in the British system and takes its lead from there. Those traditions and practices have afforded Northern Ireland's public officials a way of escaping from the sectarian conflict. The other element is that although the conflict in Northern Ireland is deep it is also narrow. Not every issue is part of the sectarian division. That means that large aspects of health, housing education and other public policies fall outside the sectarian conflict.

Conclusions: cohesion and a measure of autonomy

This chapter has dealt with the nature of policy-making in Northern Ireland, principally for those areas that do not involve, directly at least, the constitutional issue. In general, the policy network in Northern Ireland consists of a relatively small number of key actors, dominated by the Secretary of State and his ministers along with a number of senior civil servants. There are other actors, many of whom use the size of Northern Ireland to ensure access to the civil service and Ministers. In other words, the small size of Northern Ireland enables the policy network to have a considerable degree of cohesion. Organised pressure groups, with the exception on certain issues of the Churches, the Orange Order and the trade unions and employers' associations, tend not to be important. Since Direct Rule members of the minority community have been more involved.

The network has a measure of autonomy from Whitehall, and seeks to use this to protect Northern Ireland's interests as best it can. However, there are limits to this. In particular, British politicians, while recognising that Northern Ireland is in some respects different, have become less sympathetic to these arguments.

8

Understanding the Northern Ireland Problem

In this final chapter the difficult issue of the nature and resolution of the Northern Ireland problem is considered. In the last thirty years a variety of attempts have been made to devise an acceptable solution. The purpose of this chapter is to examine some of these. Since Direct Rule, there have been three major initiatives: the creation of the Power-Sharing Executive; the creation of the Northern Ireland Assembly; and the Anglo-Irish Agreement. Aspects of each of these are described in Chapter 4. Here, each will be examined in more detail of the Northern Ireland conflict and its resolution.

In addition to these three major initiatives, there has been another less radical approach – what might be described as 'keeping the lid on'. This has involved reforming various public institutions and developing policies that are designed to tackle specific dimensions, especially the economic and security aspects of the Northern Ireland problem. This more conservative approach has been adopted by various governments and is important to consider.

All of these policy initiatives are dependent on how one defines the problem. In the latter part of the chapter we shall explore some of the definitions of the problem and how the 'solutions' relate to these.

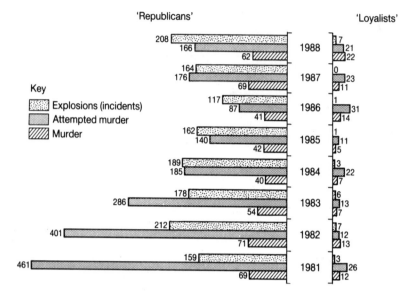

Figure 8.1 Terrorist activity, 1981–8. (*Source*: Royal Ulster Constabulary.)

'Keeping the lid on'

A major concern of British policy towards Northern Ireland has been to ensure that the problem is contained: that violence remains at an acceptable level. Figure 8.1 shows the extent of this 'success'. Its essential strategy is to ensure that each community has sufficient of its demands met that support for terrorism is to some extent restrained. The discussion in previous chapters describes many of the specifics of this approach. These include a reduction in the power of politicians in favour of bureaucrats, support for certain law and order policies (though increasingly against internment and, certainly, against capital punishment), high public expenditure and efforts to counter discrimination.

These various measures have produced a state of equilibrium in which both communities accept that their preferred option is not currently possible, but, equally, neither is the option they most oppose. The notion that Northern Ireland politics is a zero sum game, that is, if one side wins the other side must be losing, has much validity. To put it another way: if the other side is not winning, our side must be!

Nationalists were reasonably content that some effort had been made to reform the state and accepted the new institutional arrangements as an improvement on the old (Birrell 1981). But, while Unionists were no longer in charge, Nationalists were still not part of government, they were still relatively deprived economically, and their communities received the major attention from the security services.

On the other hand, Unionists were less happy with the new institutions, and their sense of alienation had increased, as evidenced by the increase in loyalist violence. In general, they resented the loss of powers under the reformed local government system. In his survey of local councillors' attitudes, Birrell found that 48 per cent of Official Unionists and 60 per cent of DUP councillors did not believe that the old local government system was in need of reform, compared with 5 per cent of Alliance councillors and 2 per cent of SDLP councillors (Birrell 1981, Table 29, p. 49).

Unionist councillors were strongly opposed to the creation of the Northern Ireland Housing Executive (66 per cent of Official Unionist councillors and 72 per cent of DUP councillors compared with 10 per cent of Alliance councillors and 2 per cent of SDLP councillors) (Birrell 1981, Table 33, p. 52). But so long as the unionist position inside the Union appeared secure, and the attentions of the police and army were directed against the IRA, this alienation was contained.

The 'keeping the lid on' strategy has a number of important drawbacks. From the British perspective, these include the continuing involvement of soldiers, with consequent high expenditure. For Unionists, there is the concern that they are not involved in the governing of Northern Ireland and the fear that events would take them into a united Ireland. For Nationalists, the absence of an agreed solution means having a heavy security presence in their areas and a feeling that they are still disadvantaged. For all, there is the fact of violence and death. These pressures have persuaded politicians to seek more radical initiatives that might increase inter-community co-operation and, with this, a resolution of the issue. What are these initiatives and why have they not succeeded?

The defeat of the Power-Sharing Executive

In the immediate post-Direct Rule period, the policy of the British government was to create a devolved government with cross-community support. As discussed in Chapter 4, a Power-Sharing Executive was formed, involving a relatively small number of Unionists, led by Brian Faulkner, the SDLP and the Alliance Party. However, the Executive was short-lived and was brought down by the Ulster Workers' Council (UWC) strike in 1974.

The strike succeeded for a variety of reasons. First, the hostility of the majority of the Protestant population to Direct Rule and the Irish dimension, in particular, cannot be under-estimated. Before the strike, faced with the might of the British and Irish governments, many Unionists felt that they had to accept the power-sharing arrangements. But these were bitterly resented, especially the Irish dimension, with much criticism being directed towards the SDLP's links with politicians in the Republic of Ireland.

The question arises as to why the SDLP felt that they had to sustain these links in the light of Protestant concerns. One explanation is provided by Bew and Patterson (1985). They argue that, within the Power-Sharing Executive, the SDLP had little influence on either security, economic or social policies. Hence, if they were to retain the support of their community, they had to have an obvious success. The creation of an Irish dimension was to provide this. The price, however, was increased Protestant alienation.

Second, and crucially, the UWC had support among electricity workers. This industry is dominated by a Protestant workforce and their commitment to the objectives of the strike were firm. The UWC, as described in Chapter 4 had organised within crucial areas of the economy.

Third, the main Unionist paramilitary force, the Ulster Defence Army (UDA), assisted the strike by intimidatory tactics, particularly during the first few days. The security forces were taken by surprise and their reaction was slow. There were accusations that their response indicated tacit support for the aims of the strike. Bew and Patterson (1985) state that there were those within the military who believed that the Executive was inevitably going to collapse and were reluctant to commit military personnel in risky ventures for little apparent gain. But generally the security forces had few options. Talk about using the Army to generate electricity supply was nonsense. When the Army was used to provide guards for petrol stations, there was a threat by the strikers that if this continued they would cease to provide any electricity supplies. There was no doubt as to where real power lay!

Fourth, some of the Unionists who had accepted positions in the Power-Sharing Executive were unhappy at using any form of strong action against the strikers. After the threats by strikers over the use of the Army to guard petrol stations, unionist members of the Executive resigned. This episode had brought them to a realisation that the strike could not be defeated with military intervention. Further, any military action against the Protestant community would have very dangerous consequences. The UWC were victorious. Power-sharing could not be imposed on the unionist community.

The importance of the strike

The strike created, for some Unionists, a myth about the use of this weapon as a means to force political change. The tactic of one-day strikes as a political protest had been employed previously, but the strike weapon had not been used in this way before. Its success greatly heartened Unionists. Moreover, given the key position of Protestant workers in the power industry, there seemed no reason why it could not be repeated, if necessary.

The second UWC strike caused rethinking on the use of political strikes. This was an attempt to secure a change in security policy and was directed at the British government. Strikes, particularly those that close down most of the economic life of the community, cause disruption and economic hardship.

It should also be remembered that the Protestant community is generally more prosperous than the Catholic one and therefore has more to lose economically. For a strike to be effective there must be a prospect of success and something definite, and important, to be gained. Without these, there will not be support among the unionist community. In this case, these conditions did not apply.

Many Unionists believed that the strike's aims were vague and not attainable. Besides, they recognised that they had fewer leverage points in that situation. It followed that there was less enthusiasm for this strike. This was true among power workers themselves, who maintained operations, assisted by a meeting with the then Secretary of State, Roy Mason. He convinced them about the effectiveness of his security policy. In addition, the security forces were much more aware of the problems of intimidation, particularly in terms of disrupting traffic, and acted swiftly and effectively. As a result, travel to and from work was maintained.

Despite these caveats, the initial UWC strike had an important impact on British and nationalist perceptions. Fisk (1983) has argued that it sapped British will to continue in Northern Ireland. This is simply not borne out by the last fifteen years. What it did do was remind British politicians that imposing solutions was a dangerous business. There are clearly limits to the loyalty of Unionists to a British government. There are also limits to the ability of a government to force on to a community initiatives that they find unacceptable. And if the strike is not always an effective weapon there are circumstances when it clearly is.

The Northern Ireland Assembly

The next case to be considered is the rolling devolution plan of James Prior, Secretary of State from September 1981 to September 1983. Prior was one of the most senior politicians to come to Northern Ireland, arriving with the ambition of making a major contribution to the resolution of the problem. At any rate, he quickly came face to face with the nature of the conflict and the violent emotions it aroused. Shortly after he took up his position, the Official Unionist MP for South Belfast, the Reverend Robert Bradford, was murdered by the Provisional IRA. Unionists were outraged and Prior was attacked at the funeral.

The Prior initiative utilised the legislation which set up the 1973 Assembly (O'Leary *et al*. 1988). His plan was that a new Assembly would be called into existence but endowed only with an advisory and consultative role until cross-community agreement was reached on devolution.

The initiative ran into difficulties with the SDLP almost from the beginning. They decided to fight the subsequent election for the new Assembly, but not to take their seats. The SDLP were increasingly concerned with the rise of Sinn Fein and this was a major factor in their thinking. Part of their response was a growing emphasis on the all-Ireland dimension, rather than attempting to resolve Northern Ireland's problems through a solution that only involved political parties within the region. This attitude contributed to the failure of the Assembly, but its full significance only emerged later.

The new Assembly met for the first time on 11 November 1983, with representatives of the two main unionist parties and the Alliance Party, together with independent Unionists in attendance. The concept of the Assembly as the initial phase of a rolling devolution was severely dented through the absence of SDLP. In addition, as O'Leary *et al*. (1988) make clear, the OUP were ambiguous about devolution, certainly about devolution on an agreed basis. Instead, the Assembly concentrated on securing a measure of political and administrative accountability from the Northern Ireland administration. The principal device used was six statutory committees, which would scrutinise the activities of Northern Ireland departments responsible for transferred matters (O'Leary *et al*. 1988, ch. 7).

These committees were modelled on the Select Committees which were created in 1979 for the House of Commons at Westminster, though there were a number of important differences. For example, the committees did not have the formal power to summon ministers or their officials. They did, however, receive draft Orders for comment and in that way could potentially influence legislation.

It is very difficult to determine the success of the scrutiny role played by the Assembly. O'Leary and his colleagues indicate that the Assembly committees did acquire information, improve the accountability of the local departments and help structure a local political agenda. Beyond that, their influence on policy matters is difficult to determine.

The appointment of the chairman of the Education Committee nearly saw the Alliance Party leave the Assembly. Their nomination for this position, John Cushnahan, was opposed by the deputy leader of the OUP, Harold McCuster, on the grounds that Cushnahan was a Catholic. This was resolved, partly by the support of Ian Paisley for Cushnahan, and the Assembly and its committees got to work. Nevertheless, on the whole, the committees did manage to create a 'team spirit', particularly between the leaders of the DUP and the Alliance Party. As O'Leary et al. (1988) state, the creation of such a team spirit is important in view of the generally adversarial nature of Northern Ireland's politics.

More importantly, the Assembly did not contribute to the resolution of the Northern Ireland problem in any significant way. The refusal of the SDLP to participate meant that the Assembly did not receive cross-community support. It was hoped that the Assembly would be so successful that eventually the SDLP would be encouraged to join it, but the time-scale necessary for this to happen was not available. With Prior's departure from the office of Secretary of State the Assembly lost its last supporter and, increasingly, events were moving in another direction – towards an Irish dimension. The signing of the Anglo-Irish Agreement saw the end of the Assembly, and it was dissolved on Monday 23 June 1986, amid unionist protests about the Agreement.

The Anglo-Irish Agreement

The third attempt at breaking the log-jam in Northern Ireland was the Anglo-Irish Agreement, signed by Garret Fitzgerald and Margaret Thatcher at Hillsborough Castle on 15 November 1985. The immediate origins of the Agreement can be traced to the meetings of Charles Haughey, then Taoiseach (Prime Minister) of the Irish Republic, and Margaret Thatcher, Prime

Minister of the United Kingdom, in 1980. At the latter of these meetings, the two Prime Ministers commissioned a number of joint studies on such matters as citizenship rights and security matters, in order 'to assist them in their special consideration of the totality of relationships within the islands'.

Dr Fitzgerald replaced Mr Haughey in June 1981, as a result of a General Election in the Republic. Nevertheless, the meetings between the two Prime Ministers continued and, in November 1981, they agreed to set up an Anglo-Irish Intergovernmental Council. This involved regular meetings of ministers and officials from both governments to discuss matters of common concern. Communications between the two governments became frosty as a result of the position of the Irish Government (now again led by Mr Haughey) on the Falklands war.

The New-Ireland Forum Report

The two governments met again in 1983, Dr Fitzgerald having replaced Mr Haughey as Taoiseach. But the most significant event in that year was the creation of the New-Ireland Forum. As earlier chapters describe, this period saw the entry of Sinn Fein into electoral politics and constitutional parties were most anxious to restrict their votes. In addition, the SDLP had come to the conclusion that Unionists would not agree to a power-sharing form of devolution and had moved towards a view that the Irish government should be explicitly involved in the government of Northern Ireland.

The Forum attempted to articulate the various views of the main constitutional nationalists about possible solutions to the Northern Ireland question. It involved the three main parties in the Republic as well as the SDLP. A number of organisations and individuals, including some prominent Unionists, gave evidence and made presentations to the Forum. In May 1984 its Report was produced.

The need to secure agreement among the four parties in the Forum shaped this document. While there was a measure of consensus about the nature and resolution of the Northern Ireland situation, fairly substantial differences in philosophy and approach still remained. Kenny (1986) has suggested that these considerations meant that the Forum Report was 'uneven, ambiguous and not entirely consistent'. For example, Chapter 5 of the Report indicates what the parties saw as the essential elements of 'a framework within which a new Ireland could emerge'. The third of these states:

> Agreement means that the political arrangements for a new and sovereign Ireland would have to be freely negotiated and agreed to by the people of the North and by the people of the South.

This was interpreted by Dr Fitzgerald and his governmental colleagues as meaning that a united Ireland could only come about as a result of agreement between the two communities. However, Unionists felt that their agreement to political structures would only be sought *after* a united Ireland had been achieved. In other words, they would be forced into a united Ireland. Kenny argues that this was also the interpretation of Mr Haughey.

Chapter 5 of the Report also spelled out the three possible solutions, as seen by the constitutional Nationalists. These were:

1. A unitary state 'achieved by agreement and consent, embracing the whole of Ireland and providing irrevocable guarantees for the protection and preservation of both the Unionist and Nationalist identities'.
2. A federal/confederal state.
3. A system of joint authority.

The first model was the preferred option of the Forum Report.

Unionists reacted with predictable hostility to the Forum Report, both main parties producing statements very critical of its analysis and recommendations. Among other political parties in the United Kingdom there was a more mixed response. James Prior, still Secretary of State, gave a muted welcome to the Report, while pointing out that there were other realities that it seemed to ignore. These included the fact that Unionists were anxious to remain within the United Kingdom. Other Conservatives were more outspoken in their opposition, while the Labour Party and the Alliance generally welcomed the Report.

However, one of the most significant comments came from Mrs Thatcher herself, when at a press conference after a meeting in December 1984 with Garret Fitzgerald she was asked for her opinion on the Forum Report and replied:

> I have made it clear . . . that a united Ireland was one solution that was out. A second solution was confederation of two states. That is out. A third solution was joint authority. That is out.

Mrs Thatcher's remarks – and more particularly the manner in which they were delivered – caused consternation in the Republic.

The changing British attitude

Despite these comments, there were a number of other influences at work. Two other significant reports were produced at about this time. One, entitled *Northern Ireland: Report of an Independent Inquiry*, emerged in November 1984 from a group of academics and other individuals interested in the Northern Ireland problem. These included Lady Briggs, whose husband had been British Ambassador in Dublin and, subsequently, was murdered by the IRA, Simon Jenkins, political editor of the *Economist*, Anthony Kenny, and two influential Northern Irish academics, A. T. Q. Stewart and Paul Arthur. The chairman was Lord Kilbrandon, former chairman of the 1973 Royal Commission on the Constitution.

The Kilbrandon Report argued that there should be a greater role for the Republic in the affairs of Northern Ireland, though there was disagreement about the extent and nature of that involvement. In effect, two models were produced: one entitled '*functional devolution*' and the other '*co-operative devolution*'. The latter focused on specific issues such as tourism, with a form of devolved government that attempted to take account of the minority concerns, but not through a power-sharing arrangement.

The former model combined two elements which were intended to have attractions for both communities. First, there was to be a real measure of devolved power to a democratically elected assembly. Second, the top tier of government in Northern Ireland would consist of an executive, consisting of the Secretary of State for Northern Ireland (or his deputy), the Minister of Foreign Affairs of the Republic of Ireland (or his deputy) and three members elected by the voters of Northern Ireland, in such a way that two of them were representative of the majority and one of the minority community. One important element in the thinking of those involved in the Inquiry (the majority) who favoured this approach was that 'co-operative devolution' could only work if it were seen as permanent. It could not be seen as a stalking horse for unification, otherwise Unionists would never accept it.

A further report that was produced in 1984 was the *Haagerup Report*, drawn up by Niels Haagerup, a Danish Euro-MP. This was completed and approved by the European Parliament, which, in the resolution accompanying the Report, declared its readiness to assume a greater responsibility for the economic and social development of Northern Ireland. The European Parliament went on to express support for the work of the Anglo-Irish Inter-governmental Conference and for growing Anglo-Irish co-operation.

All of these reports indicate that considerable backing was emerging for the idea that the way forward in Northern Ireland should involve both the Irish and British governments. There is also evidence that the US government and senior Irish-American politicians were encouraging this process.

These influences contributed to a changing British attitude to the involvement of the Irish government in Northern Ireland affairs. In addition, the British government was aware that it required the collaboration of the government of the Irish Republic in security matters if the IRA was to be contained, never mind defeated. Furthermore, spending on security in the Republic was very high. With an increasingly difficult economic situation, this might at some point become difficult to defend. The culmination of all these pressures was the signing of the Anglo-Irish Agreement.

The Agreement and its effects

The Agreement document has eleven clauses, beginning with a statement that the constitutional position of Northern Ireland would not be altered until a majority of its citizens gave their consent. It created an Inter-governmental Conference, comprising the Secretary of State for Northern Ireland and a Cabinet Minister from the Republic of Ireland, who would meet regularly to deal with political, security and related matters, legal matters, including the administration of justice, and the promotion of cross-border co-operation. The Conference would be staffed by a permanent secretariat. The Agreement also stated that in the event of a Northern Ireland Administration coming into existence, the powers devolved to it would cease to come within the remit of the Conference. The Agreement was to be subject to review after an initial period of three years, and earlier if formally requested by either government.

The signing of the Anglo-Irish Agreement initially produced a unified and deeply outraged unionist community. It is viewed by Unionists as creating joint authority over Northern Ireland by the Republic of Ireland and the United Kingdom. The British government has offered reassurances that Dublin has only a consultative, rather than executive, role, but these have been rejected by Unionists (Connolly and Loughlin 1986; Cox 1987).

The result of unionist anger, at least initially, was a wave of protest. This took several forms, including marches, a one-day strike and attempts to disrupt local government, area boards and other public agencies. Unionist MPs resigned their seats *en bloc* to force what they saw as a mini-General Election on the Anglo-Irish issue. Unionists refused to meet with ministers, and the sense of alienation that was growing within the unionist community greatly increased.

The carrot of devolved government has not persuaded Unionists to accept the Anglo-Irish Agreement. But their opposition seems less strident and a number of specific protest actions have been abandoned. Local government, at one stage the focal point of anti-Agreement protest, remains operational thanks to a series of legal manoeuvres by the Alliance Party, the reluctance of some councillors (especially those from the

OUP) to break the law and some clever tactics by government (Connolly and Knox 1988).

Instead, the debate over the appropriate tactics necessary to defeat the Agreement caused some rifts within the unionist community. The fear among a number of unionist politicians is that the Agreement will gain acceptance simply by remaining in existence over a period of time. Their ability to destroy the Agreement, without severe disruption to the economic and social fabric of Northern Ireland, as well as weakening their position within the Union, has proved to be limited.

Certain groups within the minority community were always critical of the Agreement. Sinn Fein, as well as certain republican elements in Fianna Fail (including at one stage Mr Haughey), were opposed to the Agreement. There were two reasons, namely a belief that the Agreement gave away too much on the issue of the unification of Ireland and a fear that the Agreement essentially was concerned solely with improved co-operation between the security forcs on both sides of the border.

While most Nationalists remain committed to the Agreement, a degree of disenchantment has arisen because of what they see as the lack of progress on certain issues. Initially, it appeared that their expectations would be satisfied. Orange marches were prevented from going through some Catholic areas. The Royal Ulster Constabulary (RUC) took a great deal of abuse from what had been their traditional supporters, some of whom attacked police officers and their families in their own houses. Traditional Catholic suspicion towards the police appeared to be on the way to being reversed.

Subsequently there was a measure of disappointment, largely as a result of a number of specific events in the field of law and order. The case of John Stalker, the refusal of the Government to prosecute RUC officers allegedly involved in a covert operation against IRA members that resulted in a number of deaths; the early release from prison, as well as acceptance back into the army, of a soldier found guilty of murder of a civilian; the shootings in Gibraltar of three IRA members, together with a number of other instances, caused considerable animosity among Nationalists. This led to a growth in the feeling that British justice was anti-Irish and that the Anglo-Irish Agreement was not working.

There was also some resentment among some British politicians, with a number of Conservative MPs (some of whom were always unhappy with the Agreement) calling for its abandonment. Their principal complaint was that the Irish were not sufficiently co-operative over security matters, particularly the extradition of suspected terrorists from the Republic. The case of Father Ryan was especially resented and other cases through the early part of 1990 caused further resentment.

Despite the set-backs, both governments have persisted with the Agreement. A crucial argument in its favour has been that whatever misunderstandings and differences exist, the Agreement provides a procedure for progressing, if not resolving, them. The Agreement remains, but further political movement seems to be stalemated. Unionists will not negotiate about an agreed form of devolved government while the Agreement remains, but may have little incentive if it is abandoned. Nationalists refuse to see the Agreement set aside, without an acceptable alternative in place. That is the dilemma!

Analysing the Northern Ireland problem

The Anglo-Irish Agreement remains, but so does Unionist opposition. A settlement still eludes all parties. The violence continues from both sides. Distrust and misunderstanding have not been greatly reduced.

The above discussion of the various attempts at resolving the Northern Ireland problem and the continuing conflict has forced analysts to consider whether they can identify the nature of the problem. A number of scholars have taken this approach, in particular Hunter (1982), Lijphart (1975) and Whyte (1978). The various political parties and groupings, as well as the paramilitaries, have their own analyses and accompanying solutions. What follows is a discussion of some of the more obvious ideas.

(A) Northern Ireland conflict as a religious problem

The Northern Ireland conflict is frequently described in religious terms, as a conflict between Catholics and Protestants. It is certainly true that the conflict involves division along religious lines. As discussed in earlier chapters, religion was historically a crucial element in the conflict. As Chapter 1 indicates, it continues to play an important part in life in Northern Ireland. Northern Ireland has the highest degree of commitment to religion in the United Kingdom: that is, more people in Northern Ireland view religion as important than in other parts in the United Kingdom. Attendance at church is higher than in other western countries, except the Republic of Ireland.

Political debate frequently involves religious issues. Education is one example. But more starkly, as indicated in the previous chapter, some groups see the conflict in religious terms. A number of those who support Dr Paisley believe that the conflict is about the preservation of Protestant freedom from the tyranny of Rome. A great deal of the rhetoric of some unionist politicians is cast in religious terms. The Orange Order is widely perceived as an anti-Catholic institution. As Chapter 4 records, ecumenism has been an important political issue, if not a dominant one. What is striking is that it is one at all!

The Catholic Church, particularly in its dealings with the minority community in the Republic of Ireland, is seen by Unionists as ignoring the legitimate aspirations of the Protestant people. The Church's attitude on divorce and its successful resistance to its introduction into the Republic is seen as evidence of its malign influence. The Republic of Ireland is seen by Protestants as a state dominated by a powerful and insensitive church. Within Northern Ireland, the Catholic Church has sought to protect its right to have church schools and has not always been particularly helpful to Catholics who wish to send their children to state schools. There have been attempts recently to create integrated schools, and again the Catholic church has not always offered support to these initiatives.

To declare that religion is not important in understanding the Northern Ireland conflict appears to fly in the face of the obvious. However, church leaders on both sides are quick to argue that the conflict is *not* a religious one, at least in the sense of being about religious issues. Church leaders from the mainstream churches have gone out of their way in recent years publicly to condemn violence in the strongest terms and to participate in various events, for example prayer vigils for peace and rejection of violence. Further, theological issues *per se* have not been important politically, except to a limited number of people. There is also the hope that as understanding and mutual respect among churches grows, as it has among the main churches, there will be positive benefits for the political situation in Northern Ireland.

As Lijphart (1975) points out, there is no natural relationship between political and religious cleavages. In the context of Northern Ireland, the identification of religion and political loyalties has been kept unnaturally alive for a variety of reasons. To understand the Northern Ireland situation fully one needs to know more about these reasons. In short, religious bigotry, though important, is not the whole of the story. But the religious dimension, though often neglected or understated, is an important aspect of the problem.

(B) Northern Ireland conflict as an economic problem – the class approach

Another approach has been to see the Northern Ireland problem in economic terms. There are two broad sorts of explanation that adopt this approach: one might be termed 'a class approach' while the other might be referred to as 'a deprivation approach'.

It is unlikely that marxists would avoid the issue of Northern Ireland, especially as Marx himself wrote about Ireland. Whyte (1978) distinguishes traditional and revisionist marxism. The former goes back to James Connolly and essentially argues that the basic class struggle has been obscured by sectarianism. Protestant workers have been seduced by propaganda to believe that they are in danger from a Catholic all-Ireland and have been bought off by marginal privileges.

The revisionist case is that there has been differential economic development in different parts of Ireland, with the north acquiring an industrial base while the rest of the country

remains basically agricultural. As a result, the political con-
sciousness of each part of Ireland, has differed. This view,
which is sometimes referred to as the two nations theory, is
associated with marxists sympathetic to the unionist cause. The
political implication of this perspective is that the current political division in Ireland is sensible and inevitable and will only
be abolished if and when the Republic reaches a comparable
stage of economic development.

Both approaches clearly have some merit. There has been
sectarian propaganda and discrimination. Equally, the industrialisation in Northern Ireland is – and has been – more extensive
than in other parts of Ireland. But both explanations leave
out important dimensions. Both explanations treat non-class
elements as some sort of epi-phenomenon, either as ultimately
not important or explicable through economic forces. Is this
necessarily the case? Are feelings of cultural or national identification only to be understood in class terms? If so, there is a
need to explain why Catholic workers remain nationalist and
Protestant farmers remain unionist.

One final point on the class perspective, which Lijphart
(1975) makes, is that the use of the terminology of the class
struggle is often normative, in the sense that it is used to
attempt to persuade people to 'overcome' sectarianism. The
rhetoric of the Workers Party is a good example. Its appeal is
that it maintains that sectarianism is a device which masks the
economic disadvantages of the working class as a whole in
Northern Ireland. Working-class unity is highly desirable, and
its policy is directed to this aim.

*(C) Northern Ireland conflict as an economic problem – the
deprivationist approach*

The second set of arguments that locate the problem of Northern Ireland in economics regards the conflict as centred in
the relative poverty of the people, particularly the nationalist
population, as outlined in Chapter 1. The argument is simple:
given their relative economic disadvantage many Catholics are
deeply alienated from the state and willing to support paramilitaries.

Against this there is the argument that the considerably greater public expenditure per head in Northern Ireland compared with in the rest of the United Kingdom is an expression of the commitment of the British government to alleviate poverty. In addition, significant efforts are being made to reduce inequalities of employment. There is much in this, but two counter-arguments are made. One is that the Protestant community is the main beneficiary of public expenditure. This point was made in a recent book by Rowthorn and Wayne (1988), who argue that a very high percentage of public expenditure is in those sectors of the economy, for example security, where employment is dominated by Protestants. A second argument is that a great deal of poverty and deprivation exists and can be observed. Whatever efforts have been made to alleviate poverty and unemployment in, say, West Belfast, it is not especially obvious to anyone who lives in the Divis Flats. These are inner-city areas which would throw up many social problems wherever they were located. In Northern Ireland, this is expressed in paramilitary activity.

Undoubtedly, considerable efforts are being made both with respect to anti-discrimination legislation and in support of economic development in, for example, West Belfast. The difficulty is the time required to allow these policies to succeed. But the very effort being made by government helps to persuade some people that the situation is not without hope.

That the economic perspective provides a complete explanation is a limited argument. For one thing, historically the Easter Rising of 1916 and subsequent independence occurred at a time when most Catholic grievances had been eliminated. Economic development and increased economic justice did not dispose of nationalist sentiments. Further, it is likely that had the Republic of Ireland remained as part of the United Kingdom, it would be more prosperous. But it is doubtful that such arguments would persuade its citizens to become British subjects. Nationalism, culture, traditions – political and social – matter as well as economic factors.

(D) Northern Ireland conflict as a colonial problem

One view, popular in republican circles, is the argument that Northern Ireland is a colony, held in subjection by the British. When expressed in this form it has little credibility. The vast majority of Protestants are strongly in favour of the British presence and do not see this in any way as alien and unwelcome.

Republican counter-arguments take two forms. First, the assumption is made that the Protestants are duped, and that when the British leave they will come to their senses. Again, there is no evidence for this (see O'Halloran 1987 for nationalist attitudes to Unionists). Second there is the view that the Unionists have no right to 'hold up the legitimate right of the Irish people to self determination'. Either they accept a united Ireland or leave, a view with overtones of a 'final solution'.

The colonial argument raises two sorts of questions of importance to Nationalists and Republicans. First, what is the role of the British government in Northern Ireland? Is it, as the SDLP now argues, neutral between the two communities or, as Sinn Fein would argue, an essential element in maintaining the divisions both between the two communities in Northern Ireland and between the two parts of Ireland? Is the British government simply engaged in keeping two warring factions apart or is it supportive of one side and antagonistic to the other?

The second set of questions focus around who is Irish and what rights each tradition has. One republican view holds that Unionists are not really Irish, and therefore should have no say in determining the future of the island. Most Nationalists would reject this view, arguing that a united Ireland can only come about by agreement between both communities.

(E) Northern Ireland conflict as a law and order problem

Given the prolonged violence in Northern Ireland, many of the debates about the most appropriate way forward focus on law and order. Many Unionists and some Conservatives understand the issue primarily in these terms. The problem that they see is that of a rebellious minority, intent on violence and destruction partly for political reasons but also for personal gain. In their view the solution is to adopt a tough law and order policy, the essential dimensions of which are the reintroduction of the death penalty and the use of selective detention. The objections to this approach are that it would increase nationalist alienation and, hence, ensure more support for paramilitaries. Senior police officers have recognised that the best efforts of police and army by themselves are not likely to solve the problem. Nationalist politicians go further, arguing that the existing security policy is already counter-productive. For example, they argue that house searches often are not cost-effective, generating unnecessary hostility and yielding little in the way of weapons and suspects. Government ministers are aware of their potential for stimulating conflict, but argue that searches are necessary so long as paramilitaries store weapons in houses.

Lijphart (1975) examines Mao Tse-tung's metaphor of 'the fish and the water'. The insight that emerges is useful in that it provides an understanding of the difficulties confronting the security forces in dealing with terrorists. It also indicates limits to the growth of paramilitaries in that, as Lijphart argues, both sets of terrorist groups face 'land', as one community seeks to resist the terrorism of the other.

(F) Northern Ireland conflict as a democratic problem

This perspective argues that Northern Ireland could not be regarded as a genuine democracy, because of the past electoral practices of the unionist majority. However, these practices have disappeared. Indeed, at present the main charges that Northern Ireland is governed in an undemocratic way come from the unionist community. Unionists argue that compared with other parts of the United Kingdom, citizens in Northern Ireland have less electoral influence. Local government in Northern Ireland has fewer powers than in the rest of the United Kingdom, and the people of Northern Ireland do not have the opportunity to vote for the Secretary of State and his colleagues.

One solution is increased powers for local authorities. This would be resisted by Nationalists, partly because of the unfortunate history associated with local government in Northern Ireland, and in any case is unlikely to be granted, given the attitude to local government of the current Government.

Another solution is to insist that national UK parties organise in Northern Ireland. Currently there is a campaign within Northern Ireland to persuade the Conservative and Labour parties to allow Northern Ireland-based branches to affiliate. At the 1989 Conservative Party conference, a motion enabling Northern Ireland Conservatives to organise was approved. Thus far the Labour Party has been more resistant to the idea. That the Conservatives agreed to this demand is not surprising, given its historical links with Unionism. Equally, given the Labour Party's links with the Irish community in Britain, its attitude is not surprising.

The term 'democracy' is not an unambiguous one. Does it simply mean 'rule by the majority' or are there qualitative dimensions to the definition? Accepting the first definition still leaves us with a difficulty. A number of Nationalists would argue that if a headcount is to be taken, it should be of the whole island. Irish Nationalists have tended to argue that Partition is unnatural. To quote John Bowman (1982, p. 11; the quotation is from Arthur Griffiths):

> Unlike landlocked nationalist movements elsewhere, Irish nationalism can admit of no compromise on where any new boundary line might be drawn. 'Ireland cannot shift her frontiers. The Almighty traced them beyond the cunning of man to modify'.

In short, definitions of democracy will tend to be used to support the claims of each community. Like the arguments about class, appeals to democratic practice are normative and used to support one's own particular case.

(G) Northern Ireland conflict as a bi-national problem

Finally, there is the argument that the Northern Ireland problem is one of two different nations and cultures living together but not really understanding each other. Again there seems something in this approach, but in her (1972) study Harris found a considerable degree of common culture between Catholics and Protestants. 'Despite their differences it is apparent that there is, by and large, a vast amount in common between households at the same economic level whatever their religious affiliation' (Harris 1972, p. ix). However, she goes on to make the point that in the community she studied there is not much contact between people of different religious denominations.

Harris's concern was with the totality of social life, but culture may be a multi-dimensional concept. If it can be broken into constituent elements, then divisions can be identified. For example, Lijphart (1975) makes the point that the political culture of both communities is separate and sharply demarcated. Many Nationalists would argue that their political culture has been deemed illegitimate for many years. For them to espouse a desire for Irish unification was by itself viewed as unacceptable. The institutions of the state were not neutral but hostile to this aspiration. The state's symbols were those of Unionism, while Nationalist symbols, for example the Gaelic language and games, were regarded with suspicion. This is a theme which has been sounded increasingly by nationalist politicians and which found favour in the Anglo-Irish Agreement.

Unionists would argue that the idea of unification with a Gaelic and Catholic Ireland holds little attraction for them. Such a concept is culturally unacceptable to them. When politicians from the Republic emphasise this aspect of Irishness, it simply reinforces unionist resistance.

It has to be stressed that, as the previous chapter illustrates, there is no simple identification to be made of Catholics with Irishness, on the one hand, and Protestants with Britishness on the other. In any case, the concepts of Irishness and Britishness are not without their ambiguity. Another complication is that, while the division between both communities is deep, there are those who cross it. The alluring idea already mentioned that some Catholics in Northern Ireland are anti-unionist and not anti-Union is one that deserves consideration. However important the culture argument is, it needs greater refinement and development'.

Conclusions: an intractable problem

These, then, represent some of the ways in which the Northern Ireland issue is conceptualised. The difficulty is that no one way is adequate, and all ways are open to various interpretations. The crucial element in the Northern Ireland problem is that a number of differences are mutually reinforcing.

After an extensive review of the literature, Lijphart (1975, p. 96) concludes that 'Northern Ireland can be best understood as a plural society, our understanding complemented by images of the country as a colony, a fragment society and a majority dictatorship'.

The point about determining how the issue is understood is that it provides a guide to generating the most appropriate and sensible policies to resolving (or at least ameliorating) the problem. Lijphart takes this step, going on to draw policy implications from his analysis. Economic and electoral reforms, though valuable, are not a solution, as they do not address the fundamental issues. Decolonisation (that is, British withdrawal), Lijphart suggests, may be considered as part of a solution. But he ultimately rejects it on the grounds that it has too many loose ends to be practical.

A number of groups and individuals in Britain have started to advocate this position, but so far it does not have serious support among policy-makers. The problem is that it is likely to lead to considerable violence, violence that may not be contained within Northern Ireland, or indeed Ireland. Faced with such violence, Britain may be forced by international opinion to intervene. Given such uncertainties, the case for the British staying put seems preferable.

Suggested policy initiatives

Lijphart examines three further policy initiatives. First, there have been suggestions that greater integration might be fostered between the communities in Northern Ireland. This Lijphart dismisses as wishful thinking. Despite this, there are signs that those who desire greater integration are making some progress. For example, in education, where there has traditionally been a separated system, there have been limited developments in integrated schooling. There is little likelihood of integration increasing much before the violence ends. But if the idea that many in the minority are anti-unionist but not opposed to the Union *per se* has some validity, there would be much merit in encouraging integration. Over time, hostilities may be reduced with growing contacts between the communities.

One policy solution that has developed within the unionist community is that there should be greater integration between Northern Ireland and the rest of the United Kingdom. This view is held by those Unionists who identify with Britain rather than Ulster. It would end uncertainty about Northern Ireland's constitutional position, and this would encourage the development of 'normal' politics. They further argue that integration would safeguard the position of Catholics, in that they would be part of the United Kingdom and would be governed not by Unionists but by British ministers. A main nationalist argument against this position is that it pretends that Northern Ireland is just like any other part of the United Kingdom, and this is clearly not the case. Other Unionists worry about the prospect that control of their future would pass to the British, whom a growing number of them distrust.

Second, Lijphart considers the possibility of power-sharing, that is, a system in which both communities share governmental posts. This solution has been associated with writers on consociational theory. In a consociational democracy, political stability is achieved in a culturally divided society by an agreement among the elites of the sub-cultural groupings to join in the government of the country. This involves some sort of grand coalition rule and agreement on an equitable distribution of appointments, etc.

Lijphart, following Richard Rose, is sceptical as to whether this is a viable solution for Northern Ireland. Basically, the conditions necessary for power-sharing do not exist. Lijphart identifies three in particular. First, there needs to be a multiple balance of power – for example three groupings in which none has a clear majority. In Northern Ireland there is a permanent imbalance of power. Second, the Protestant community does not accept the power-sharing model. Its standards and traditions of democracy are drawn from Britain and the British model. In such a system, power-sharing is viewed as un-British and undemocratic. Finally, there usually needs to be a degree of overarching loyalty, normally to 'the nation'. This, of course, is precisely what is missing in Northern Ireland.

Rose had articulated many of these problems in his seminal book *Governing Without Consensus*, published in 1971, and his forecast that a power-sharing government, consisting not of the 'grand coalition' but of unionist moderates and nationalists, would be susceptible to an 'ultra rising against the regime' (Rose 1971, pp. 390–1) proved accurate.

The third solution that Lijphart offers is a new version of partition. He complains that this solution has not been adequately considered, but it has recently been argued by Liam Kennedy (1986). Lijphart briefly discusses two ideas. The most extreme version would involve separating out the two communities, with the Catholics moving to the western part of Northern Ireland and presumably ultimately joining the Republic.

In a sense this was what many Catholics thought would happen in 1920, with the Boundary Commission ceding large parts of what are now Northern Ireland to what was then the Irish Free State. A less extreme version of partition would be to enhance local government by giving it more powers and making it coterminous with sectarian divisions. For both versions Lijphart accepts that there would be grave difficulties, but argues that the idea is at least worth examining. One major obstacle is that it is an idea that no serious politician supports. Nor is there any support for the idea within Northern Ireland. Many Unionists would worry that any major reduction in the borders of Northern Ireland would pose questions about its long-term viability. As already discussed, many Nationalists' image of Ireland embraces the whole of the island.

The continuing challenge

Faced with the range of 'solutions', all of which seem to have serious limitations, it is not surprising that the low-key approach discussed earlier is so attractive. Clearly no solution has as yet emerged.

In the meantime, the existence of the Anglo-Irish Agreement has introduced a new element into the situation. It is possible that Unionists, fearing the further erosion of their position, might come forward with a package for devolved government that would be acceptable to Nationalists. It is equally possible that Unionists' fears about the ultimate intentions of Nationalists would prevent such a move. There have been signs of both approaches developing within the Unionist community. It is difficult to predict the way forward.

One is reminded of Churchill's famous remark about the integrity of the Irish quarrel surviving no matter what worldly upheaval occurs. That perhaps is the measure of the challenge facing politicians who aspire to resolve the Northern Ireland problem.

References

Akenson, D. H. (1973) *Education and Enmity: The History of Schooling in Northern Ireland*, David and Charles.

Arthur, P. (1984) *Government and Politics of Northern Ireland*, Longman (second edition).

Arthur, P. and Jeffrey, K. (1988) *Northern Ireland Since 1968*, Blackwell.

Barton, B. (1988) *Brookeborough: The Making Of A Prime Minister*, Queen's University Institute of Irish Studies.

Beckett, J. C. (1981) *The Making of Modern Ireland 1603–1923*, Faber.

Bell, E. (1985) 'What people should know about the role of the Civil Service in Northern Ireland since 1968', *Belfast Telegraph*, 29 Jan., p. 12.

Bell, P. N. (1987) 'Direct rule in Northern Ireland', Chapter 7 in Rose pp. 189–226.

Benson, J. K. (1982) 'A framework for policy analysis' in Rodgers, Whitten and Associates (eds) pp. 137–76.

Bew, P., Gibbon, P. and Patterson, H. (1979) *The State in Northern Ireland, 1921–1972*, Manchester University Press.

Bew, P. and Patterson, H. (1985) *The British State and the Ulster Crises: From Wilson to Thatcher*, Verso.

Birrell, D. (1981) *Local Government Councillors in Northern Ireland*, CSSP Studies No. 83, University of Strathclyde.

Birrell, D. and Murie, A. (1980) *Policy and Government in Northern Ireland: Lessons of Devolution*, Gill and Macmillan.

Bishop, P. and Mallie, E. (1987) *The Provisional IRA*, Heinemann.

Blease (Lord) (1984) *The Trade Union Movement in Northern Ireland*, Ulster Polytechnic

Boal, F. W. (1987) *Belfast: The Physical and Social Dimensions of a Regional City*, in Buchanan and Walker (eds).

Boal, F. W. and Douglas, J. N. H. (1982) *Integration and Division*, Academic Press.

Bowman, J. (1982) *De Valera and The Ulster Question 1917–1973*, Clarendon Press.

Brady, C., O'Dowd, M. and Walker, B. (eds) (1989) *Ulster: An Illustrated History*, Batsford.

Brett, C. (1986) *Housing a Divided Community*. Institute of Public Administration.

Bruce, S. (1986) *God Save Ulster: The Religion and Politics of Paisleyism*, Clarendon Press.

Buchanan, R. H. (1987) 'Province, city and people', in Buchanan and Walker (eds).

Buchanan, R. H. and Walker, B. M. (eds) (1987) *Province, City and People: Belfast and its Region*, Greystone Books.

Buckland, P. (1979) *The factory of Grievances: Devolved Government in Northern Ireland 1921–39*, Gill and Macmillan.

Buckland, P. (1981) *A History of Northern Ireland*, Gill and Macmillan.

Bustead, M. A. (1972) *Northern Ireland: Geographical Aspects of a Crisis*, University of Oxford Press, School of Geography Research Paper No. 3.

Bustead, M. A. and Mason, H. (1971) 'Local government reform in Northern Ireland', *Irish Geography*, vol. 31, no. 3, pp. 315–23.

Callaghan, J. (1973) *A House Divided*, Collins.

Cameron Report (1969) *Disturbances in Northern Ireland*, Report of the Commission appointed by the Governor of Northern Ireland, HMSO (Belfast), Cmd. 532.

Canny, N. (1989) 'Early modern Ireland, c. 1500–1700', in Foster (ed.) pp. 104–60.

Clarke, A. (1984) 'The colonisation of Ulster and the rebellion of 1641', Chapter 12 in Moody and Martin (eds) pp. 189–203.

Clarke, L. (1987) *Broadening the Battlefield; the H-Blocks and the Rise of Sinn Fein*, Gill and Macmillan.

Compton, P. (1987) 'Population', Chapter 12 in Buchanan and Walker (1987).

Connolly, M. (1983) *Central-Local Relations in Northern Ireland: A Report to ESRC*, Ulster Polytechnic.

Connolly, M. (1983) 'What happens when the government takes over? Local government in Northern Ireland', *Local Government Policy Making*, vol. 10, no. 2, Nov., pp. 7–20.

Connolly, M. (1986) 'Controlling local government expenditure: the case of Northern Ireland', *Public Administration*, vol. 64, no. 1, Spring, pp. 83–96.

Connolly, M. and Knox, C. (1986) 'Reflections on the 1985 local government elections in Northern Ireland', *Local Government Studies*, vol. 12, no. 2. pp. 15–29.

Connolly, M. and Knox, C. (1988) 'Recent political difficulties of local government in Northern Ireland, *Policy and Politics*, vol. 16, no. 2, pp. 89–97.

Connolly, M. and Loughlin, J. (1986) 'Reflections on the Anglo-Irish Agreement', *Government and Opposition*, vol. 21, no. 2, pp. 146–60.

Connolly, M. and Loughlin, S. (eds) (1990) *Public Policy in Northern Ireland: Adoption or Adaption?*, Policy Research Institute.

Connolly, M. and McAlister, D. (1988) 'Public expenditure in Northern Ireland', Chapter 10 in *Public Domain Yearbook 1988*, Public Finance Foundation.

Continuous Household Survey (1989) *PPRU Monitor No. 1/89, Religion*, Policy Planning and Research Unit, Department of Finance and Personnel.

Cormack, R. J. and Osbourne, R. D. (eds) (1983) *Religion, Education and Employment in Northern Ireland*, Appletree Press.

Cowan, R. (1982) 'Belfast's hidden planners', *Town and Country Planning*, June 1982, pp. 163–5.

Cox, W. Harvey (1987) 'The Anglo-Irish Agreement', *Parliamentary Affairs*, vol. 40, no. 1, Jan, pp. 80–97.

Darby, J. (1976) *Conflict in Northern Ireland: The Development of a Polarised Community*, Gill and Macmillan.

Darby, J. (1983) *Northern Ireland: Background to the Conflict*, Appletree Press.

Darby, J. (1983) 'Historical Background', Chapter 1 in Darby, J.

Darby, J. (1985) 'Controls on conflict', *L'Irlande Politique et Sociale: Le Conflit En Irlande Du Nord*, vol. 1, no. 1, pp. 77–86.

Darby, J. and Williamson, A. (eds) (1978) *Violence and the Social Services in Northern Ireland*, Heinemann Educational Books.

Devlin, P. (1981) *Yes, We Have No Bananas*, Appletree Press.

Ditch, J. (1977) 'Direct Rule and Northern Ireland', *Administration*, Winter, pp. 328–37.

Doherty, C. (1989) *Ulster Before the Normans: Ancient Myth and Early History*, in Brady, O'Dowd and Walker pp. 13–43.

Edwards, R. D. (1977) *Patrick Pearse: The Triumph of Failure*, Faber.

Electricity Supply in Northern Ireland Energy Committee, House of Commons, Session 1987–88, Fifth Report, 9 November 1988, HMSO.

Elliot, M. (1982) *Partners in Revolution: The United Irishman and France*, Yale University Press.

Elliott, M. (1989) *Wolfe Tone: Prophet of Irish Independence*, Yale University Press.

Elliot, R. S. P. and Hickie, J. (1971) *Ulster: A Case Study in Conflict Theory*, Longman.

Equality of Opportunity in Employment: New proposals, Department of Economic Development, 1988.

Family Expenditure Survey, *PPRU Monitor Number 3/88*, Policy Planning and Research Unit, Department of Finance and Personnel (September) 1988.

Fisk, R. (1983) *In Time Of War*, Andre Deutsch.

Foster, R. F. (1988) *Modern Ireland 1600–1972*, Allen Lane, Penguin.

Foster, R. F. (ed.) (1989) *The Oxford History of Ireland*, Oxford University Press.

Further and Higher Education in Northern Ireland, Education, Science and Arts Committee, House of Commons, Session 1982–3, Second Report, 9 May 1983, HMSO.

Gallagher, T. and O'Connelll, J. (1983) *Contemporary Irish Studies*, Manchester University Press.

Graham, D. (1983) 'Discrimination in Northern Ireland: the failure of the Fair Employment Agency', *Critical Social Policy*, no. 9, pp. 40–54.

Green, A. (1979) *Devolution and Public Finance: Stormont from 1921 – 1972* (Studies in Public Policy No. 49), Centre for Study of Public Policy, University of Strathclyde.

Green, E. R. R. (1984) *The Great Famine*, in Moody and Martin (eds) pp. 263–74.

Greer, J. and Jess, P. (1987) *Town and Country Planning*, in Buchanan and Walker (eds).

Hadfield, B. (1990) 'The role of MPs in the policy process in Northern Ireland', Chapter 4 in Connolly and Loughlin (eds).

Harbinson, J. F. (1973) *The Ulster Unionist Party 1882–1973. Its Development and Organisation*, Blackstaff Press.

Harkness, D. (1983) *Northern Ireland Since 1920*, Helicon.

Harris, R. (1972) *Prejudice and Tolerance in Ulster: A Study of Neighbours and 'Strangers' in a Border Community*, Manchester University Press.

Harrison, R. T. (1986) 'Industrial development policy and the restructuring of the Northern Ireland economy, *Environment and Planning C: Government and Policy*, vol. 4, pp. 53–70.

Harvey, S. and Rea, D. (1982) *The Northern Ireland Economy with*

Particular Reference to Industrial Development, Pirc, Ulster Polytechnic.

Hewitt, C. (1982) 'Catholic grievances, Catholic nationalism and violence in Northern Ireland during The Civil Rights period: a reconsideration', *British Journal of Sociology*, vol. 32, no. 3, September, pp. 362–80.

Hopkinson, M. (1988) *Green Against Green: The Irish Civil War*, Gill and Macmillan.

Hunter, J. (1982) *An Analysis of the Conflict in Northern Ireland*, in Rea, D. (ed.) pp. 9–59.

Jackson, P. (ed.) (1985) *Implementing Government Policy Initiatives*, RIPA.

Johnson, J. H. (1970) 'Reorganization of local government in Northern Ireland', *Area*, no. 4, pp. 17–21.

Keating, M. and Midwinter, A. (1983) *The Government of Scotland*, Mainstream Press.

Kee, R. (1976) *The Most Distressful Country*, Quartet.

Kennedy, D. (1988) *The Widening Gulf: Northern Attitudes to the Independent Irish State*, Blackstaff Press.

Kennedy, L. (1986) *Two Ulsters: A Case For Repartition*, Queens University, Belfast.

Kennedy, S. and Birrell, D. (1978) *Housing*, in Darby, J. and Williamson, A.

Kenny, A. (1986) *The Road to Hillsborough: The Shaping of the Anglo-Irish Agreement*, Pergamon Press.

Knox, C. (1989) 'Local government in Northern Ireland', *Public Money and Management*, vol. 9, no. 2, pp. 59–63.

Laffan, M. (1983) *The Partition of Ireland 1911–1925*, Dublin Historical Association.

Lijphart, A. (1975) Review article, 'The Northern Ireland problem: cases, theories, and solutions', *British Journal of Political Science*, vol. 5, no. 1, June pp. 83–106.

Local Government Consultative Paper (1988) Department of the Environment for Northern Ireland, November.

Lyons, F. S. L. (1973) *Ireland since the Famine*, Fontana (2nd edn).

MacDonagh, O. (1988) *The Hereditary Bondsman: Daniel O'Connell 1775–1829*, Weidenfeld and Nicolson.

Macrory Report (1970) *Review Body on Local Government in Northern Ireland Report*, HMSO.

Malpass, P. and Murie, A. (1982) *Housing Policy and Practice*, Macmillan.

McAllister, I. (1971) *The SDLP*, Macmillan.

McAllister, I. (1983) 'Political parties: traditional and modern', Chapter 3 in Darby, pp. 61–78.

McCrudden, C. (1983) *The Experience of the Legal Enforcement of The Fair Employment (Northern Ireland) Act 1976*, in Cormack and Osbourne (eds).

Matthew Report (1983) *Belfast Regional Survey and Plan: Recommendations and Conclusions* (Cmd 451), HMSO.

Ministry of Health and Social Services (MHSS) (1973) *Report and Recommendations of the Working Party on Discrimination in the Private Sector of Employment*, HMSO.

Moloney, E. and Pollock, A. (1986) *Paisley*, Poolbeg.

Moody, T. W. (1987) *Fenianism, Home Rule and the Land War*, in Moody and Martin (eds) pp. 275–93.

Moody, T. W. and Martin, F. X. (1987) *The Course of Irish History*, Mercier.

Mullen, K. (1988a) 'The Fair Employment (Northern Ireland) Act 1976', *Equal Opportunities International*, pp. 1–9.

Mullen, K. (1988b) 'Reforming anti-discrimination legislation in Northern Ireland', *Public Money and Management*, vol. 8, nos. 1–2, pp. 69–72.

Murie, A. (1985) 'What the country can afford? Housing under the Tories 1979–83' in Jackson (ed) pp. 169–88.

Needs Assessment Study (1979), HMSO.

Nelson, S. (1984) *Ulster's Uncertain Defenders: Loyalists and the Northern Ireland Conflict*, Appletree Press.

Northern Ireland Economic Council (1987), *Northern Ireland Economic Council Annual Report 1987/88*, Report Number 67, October.

Northern Ireland Economic Council (1981), Northern Ireland Economic Report Number 19: *The Northern Ireland Construction Industry*, March.

Northern Ireland Economic Council (1981), Northern Ireland Economic Report Number 21: *Public Expenditure Priorities: Housing*, May.

Northern Ireland Economic Council (1985), Northern Ireland Economic Report Number 48: *Review of Recent Developments in Housing Policy*, February.

Northern Ireland Economic Council (1989), Northern Ireland Economic Report: *Economic Assessment*, Number 75, April.

Northern Ireland Economic Council (1989), Northern Ireland Economic Report Number 42: *Public Expenditure Priorities: Overall Review*, March.

Northern Ireland: Report of an Independent Inquiry, (Chairman Lord Kilbrandon), The Independent Inquiry 1984.

O'Connor, U. (1984) *Celtic Dawn*, Black Swan.

O'Corrain, D. (1989) *Prehistoric and Early Christian Ireland*, in Foster (ed.) pp. 51–2.

O'Farrell, F. (1981) *Daniel O'Connell*, Gill and Macmillan.

O'Halloran, C. (1987) *Partition and the Limits of Irish Nationalism*, Gill and Macmillan.

O'Leary, C., Elliot, S. and Wilford, R. (1988) *The Northern Ireland Assembly 1982–1986: A Constitutional Experiment*, Hurst St Martin's.

O'Malley, P. (1983) *The Uncivil Wars: Ireland Today*, Blackstaff Press.

O'Neill, T. (1972) *The Autobiography of Terence O'Neill*, Hart-Davis.

Oliver, I. (1987) *Police, Government and Accountability*, Macmillan.

Oliver, J. (1976) *Working at Stormont*, Institute of Public Administration, Dublin.

Osbourne, R. D. (1982) *Equality of Opportunity and Discrimination: The Case of Religion in Northern Ireland Administration*, vol. 29, no. 4, pp. 331–5.

Osbourne, R. D. and Cormack, R. J. (1989) 'Fair employment: towards reform in Northern Ireland', *Policy and Politics*, vol. 17, no. 4, pp. 287–94.

Osbourne, R. D., Cormack, R. J. and Millar, R. L. (eds) (1987) *Education and Policy in Northern Ireland*, Policy Research Institute.

Patten, C. (1985) 'Housing policy in Northern Ireland: an interview with the Minister, Chris Patten', *Housing Review*, vol. 34, no. 5, Sept.–Oct., pp. 155–9.

Phoenix, E. (1989) 'Northern Ireland: from birth pangs to disintegration, 1920–1972' in Brady, O'Dowd and Walker (eds) pp. 182–216.

Policy Planning Research Unit (1989) PPRU Monitor Number 1, Religion, Department of Finance and Personnel.

Poole, M. A. (1982) *Religious Residential Segregation in Urban Northern Ireland*, in Boal and Douglas pp. 281–308.

Quigley, W. G. H. (1987) 'The public expenditure system in Northern Ireland', *Business Outlook and Economic Review*, vol. 2, no. 2, July, pp. 29–32.

Rea, D. (ed.) (1982) *Political Co-operation in Divided Societies*, Gill and Macmillan.

Rees, M. (1980) 'Direct Rule in practice', *Belfast Telegraph*, 11 March.

Report and Recommendations of the Working Party on Discrimination in the Private Sector of Employment (1973), HMSO.

Rhodes, R. (1981) *Control and Power in Central-Local Relations*, Gower.

Rhodes, R. (1985) 'Power-dependence, policy communities and inter-governmental relations', *Public Administration Bulletin*, No. 59, Dec., pp. 4–31.

Rhodes, R. (1988) *Beyond Westminster and Whitehall*, Unwin.

Rodgers, D., Whitten, D. and Associates (1982) *Interorganizational Coordination*, Iowa State University Press.

Rose, R. (1971) *Governing Without Consensus: An Irish Perspective*, Faber.

Rose, R. (1976) *Northern Ireland: A time of Choice*, Macmillan.

Rose, R. (1982) *Understanding the United Kingdom: The Territorial Dimension in Government*, Longman.

Rose, R. (1987) *Ministers and Ministers: A Functional Analysis*, Clarendon Press.

Rowthorn, B. and Wayne, N. (1988) *Northern Ireland: The Political Economy of Conflict*, Polity.

Saunders, P. (1983) *The 'Regional State': A Review of the Literature and Agenda for Research*, Working Paper 35, Urban and Regional Studies, University of Sussex.

Simms, K. (1989) *The Norman Invasion and the Gaelic Recovery*, in Foster (ed.).

Sinclair, K. (1986) 'A review of recent legal decisions in Northern Ireland affecting local authorities', *Local Government Studies*, vol. 12, no. 5, Sept.–Oct.

Singleton, D. (1982a) ' "Council house" sales in Northern Ireland', *Housing Review*, March–April, pp. 43–5.

Singleton, D. (1982b) 'Housing a divided community, *Housing Review*, May–June, pp. 77–81.

Singleton, D. (1985) 'Housing and planning in Northern Ireland: problems of a divided community', *Policy and Politics*, vol. 13, no. 3, pp. 305–26.

Smyth, C. (1987) *Ian Paisley: Voice of Protestant Ulster*, Scottish Academic Press Ltd.

Stewart, A. T. Q. (1981) *Edward Carson*, Gill and Macmillan

Stewart, A. T. Q. (1986) *The Narrow Ground: Patterns of Ulster History*, Pretani Press (first published 1977).

The Sunday Times Insight Team, (1972) *Ulster*, Penguin.

Text of a Communique (1969) Cmnd. 4178, HMSO.

Todd, J. (1987) 'Two traditions in unionist political culture', *Irish Political Studies*, vol. 2, pp. 1–26.

Townshend, C. (1983) *Political Violence in Ireland: Government and Resistance Since 1848*, Oxford University Press.

Wallace, M. (1971) *Northern Ireland: 50 Years of Self Government*, David and Charles.

Wallis, R., Bruce, S. and Taylor, D. (1986) 'No Surrender'. Paisleyism and the Politics of Ethnic Identity in Northern Ireland, The Queen's University, Belfast.

Walsh, D. P. J. (1983) The Use and Abuse of Emergency Legislation in Northern Ireland, The Cobden Trust.

White, B. (1984) John Hume: Statesman of The Troubles, Blackstaff Press.

White, B. (1986) 'Bias in jobs: why the Government is getting tough', Belfast Telegraph, 3 Oct., p. 9.

Whyte, J. (1978) 'Interpretations of the Northern Ireland problem: an appraisal', Economic and Social Review, vol. 9, no. 4, 257–82.

Whyte, J. (1983) How Much Discrimination Was There Under the Unionist Regime, 1921–68?, in Gallagher and O'Connell.

Whyte, J. H. (1980) Church and State In Modern Ireland 1923–1979, Gill and Macmillan, 2nd edn.

Woodham-Smith, C. (1962) The Great Hunger: Ireland 1845–9, Hamish Hamilton.

Wright, F. (1972) 'Protestant ideology in politics in Ulster', European Journal of Sociology, vol. 14, pp. 213–80.

Index

Act of Union, 19
Adams, Gerry, 111
agriculture, 9, 10, 23, 154
Akenson, D. H., 42, 126
Alliance Party, 62, 80, 94, 99, 108–9,
    140, 143, 144, 149
Anglo-Irish Agreement, 68ff., 77,
    106–7, 114, 121, 134, 137,
    144ff., 159
Antrim, 4, 31
Apprentice Boys, 17, 58
area boards, 79
Armagh, 4, 31, 39
Arthur, P., 15, 39, 41, 48, 49, 98, 99,
    104, 108, 147
Arthur, P. and Jeffrey, K., 108, 110
Assembly, 69, 96, 137, 142ff.

Baldwin, Stanley, 34, 42
Bann river, 7
Barton, B., 41
Battle of Aughrim, 17
Battle of the Boyne, 16–18
Battle of the Somme, 27
BBC, 78
Beckett, J. C., 23
Belfast, 6, 23, 31, 39, 57, 58
Bell, P. N., 88
Benson, J. K., 116
Bew, P. and Patterson, H., 61, 62,
    98, 140
bi-confessional parties, 108
Birrell, D., 9, 31, 46, 82, 90, 98, 102,
    127, 131, 139

Bishop, P. and Maillie, E., 110
Black and Tans, 28
Blease, Lord, 119
Boal, F. W., 6
Boundary Commission, 33, 34, 162
Bowman, J., 37
Bradford, Robert, 143
Briggs, Lady, 147
British Army, 1, 27, 58, 139, 141
Brooke, Peter, 70
Brookeborough, 40, 41, 45, 47
Browne, Noel, 37–8
Bruce, S., 105
Buchanan, R. H., 7
Buckland, P., 26, 35, 36, 37, 41, 44,
    51, 61. 65
Bustead, M. A., 51

Caledon, 55
Callaghan, J., 55, 58–9
Cameron Report, 50, 56
Campaign for Social Justice, 48, 49,
    54
Canny, N., 14
Carson, 26, 34, 40
Castlereagh, 107
Catholic Emancipation Act 1829, 21
Cavan, 4, 39
CBI-NI, 120
cease-fire, 65
Charles I, 16
Chief Constable, 83, 84
Church of Ireland, 8, 24
civil rights, 54

civil rights marches, 54
civil servants (UK), 59, 92
Civil War, 34
Clarke, A., 15
Clarke, L., 67
Collins, Michael, 28, 34, 35, 37
colonialism, 156, 160
community relations, 58
Compton, P., 7
confessional parties, 108
Connaught, 13
Connolly, James, 27, 153
Connolly, M., 76, 80
Connolly, M. and Knox, C., 77, 106, 150
Connolly, M. and Loughlin, J., 149
Constitutional Conference, 65
Constitution of Irish Republic, 37, 38
Cosgrave, 34, 42
Council of Ireland, 31
Cowan, R., 128
Cox, W. Harvey, 149
Craig, James, 26, 30, 32, 33, 34, 35, 37, 40, 42
Craig, William, 55, 56, 65
Cromwell, 16
Currie, Austin, 55
Cushnahan, 144

Dail Eireann, 33, 34
Darby, J., 15, 50, 51
de Valera, Eamon, 33, 37, 38
decolonisation, 160
democracy, 157–8
Democratic Unionist Party (DUP), 64, 65, 80, 101, 102, 103–4, 106, 107, 139, 144
demography, 3–5
Department of Agriculture Northern Ireland (DANI), 92, 94, 124
Department of Economic Development (DED), 85, 86, 94
Department of Education for Northern Ireland (DENI), 80, 94
Department of Environment for Northern Ireland (DOENI), 73, 80, 94
and NIHE 81–2, 129–31
Department of Finance, 90, 91, 92, 93
Department of Finance and

Personnel (DFP), 89, 93, 94, 121, 122ff.
Department of Health and Social Services for Northern Ireland (DHSS), 80, 90, 94
Departments (Northern Ireland) Order 1983, 93
depoliticisation, 78, 97
Dermot, 12–13
Derry, 15, 17, 51, 55, 58, 61
Devlin, P. 44, 99
Diplock, Lord Justice, 66
Direct Rule, 61, 62, 89, 92ff., 94, 97, 127, 137, 140
dirty protest, 67
discrimination, 41, 50ff., 138, 155
debate about, 52ff.
Ditch, J., 61
Divis Flats, 155
Doherty, C., 12
Donegal, 4, 21
Down, 4, 31
Drogheda, 16
Dublin, 13, 27, 69
Dungannon, 51

Easter Rising 1916, 27–8, 155
economy, 9–11, 44, 46
and Northern Ireland problem, 153ff.
Education, 46, 115, 126, 133, 136
Education Act 1923, 118
education and library boards 73, 79, 80
Edwards, R. D., 27
Elected Authorities (NI) Bill, 78
elections, 50
Elizabeth I, 14
Elliot, M., 19
Elliot, R. S. P. and Hickie, J., 56
employment, 51, 52, 54
employers' association, 120
engineering, 23, 154
England, 4, 9, 11, 15, 123
European Community, 68, 125

Fair Employment Agency (FEA), 84ff., 134–5
Fair Employment Commission (FEC), 86–7
Fair Employment Tribunal, 87
famine, 22
Faulkner, Brian, 57, 103, 140

Feakle Talks, 65
Fenians, 24
Fermanagh, 4, 7, 31, 34, 51, 72
Fermanagh and South Tyrone, 67
Fianna Fail, 150
Fire Authority, 73
Fisk, R., 142
Fitt, Gerry, 112
Fitzgerald, Garret, 69, 144
Flight of the Earls, 15
Foreign Office, 68, 121
Foster, R. F., 14, 15, 16, 41
Free Presbyterian, Church, 104
Free State, 28, 33, 34, 37
  constitution of 1937, 37–8
  neutrality in Second World War,
  38, 45
French Revolution, 19

Gaelic, 14
Gardiner, Lord, 66
Gladstone, 24–5
Government of Ireland Act 1920, 3,
  28, 30ff.
Graham, D., 86
Grattan, 19
Great Britain, 4
Great Famine, 22–3
Green, E., 22
Greer, J. and Jess, P., 6
Griffiths, Arthur, 28

Haagerup, Neils, 148
Hadfield, B., 95
Harbinson, J. F., 104, 117
Harkness, D., 32, 35, 39, 45, 46, 47,
  48, 53, 57, 60, 61
Harland and Wolff, 125
Harris, R., 158, 159
Harrison, R. T., 10
Harvey, S. and Rea, D., 9
Haughey, Charles, 69, 144, 145, 150
health, 115, 133, 136
health and social services boards, 73,
  79, 80
Health Services Act, 1948, 46
Heath, Ted, 61
Henry II, 12–13
Henry VIII, 13–14
Hewitt, C., 52
Home Office, 91
Home Rule, 23–5, 30
Hopkinson, M., 34

housing, 128ff., 136
  discrimination and 50–1, 54, 55, 56
  state of 10–11, 132
Housing Finance Order (NI) 1977,
  81
Housing (NI) Order 1981, 81
Hume, John, 57, 112
hunger strikes, 67
Hunt Report, 83
Hunt, Lord, 59, 60, 83
Hunter, J., 151

IBA, 78
industrial development, 115
Inter-governmental Conference, 69
Internees, 65
Internment, 43, 60, 61, 66
intregration with UK, 161
  introduction of 87
Irish Americans, 23, 68, 85
Irish chiefs, 13, 14
Irish Parliamentary Party, 23–4
Irish Republican Army, (IRA), 23,
  28, 41, 42, 46, 47, 57, 58, 60,
  62, 101, 103, 109, 110ff., 139
  Official IRA, 58, 60, 110
  Provisional IRA, 58, 60, 65, 67,
  77, 84, 110ff.
Irish Republican Brotherhood, 23–4

James II, 16–17
Jenkins, Simon, 147
Joint Exchequer Board, 32
junior ministers, 87

Kee, R., 13, 14, 20
Kennedy, D., 37, 40, 41
Kenny, A., 145, 146, 147
Kilbrandon, Lord, 147
  Report, 147–8
Kinsale, 14
Knox, C., 77, 78, 106, 150

labour market, 52ff.
Laffan, M., 23, 34
Land League, 24
Land War, 24
law and order, 42ff., 66ff., 82, 116,
  138, 156ff.
Lemass, Sean, 48
Lijphart, A., 151, 152, 154, 157, 159,
  160, 161
linen, 23

Lisburn, 39
Lloyd George, 28, 30, 33, 34
local government, 71ff., 97
  1985 election, 111
  finance, 76–7
  franchise, 50–2, 56
  functions, 75
  and Housing Executive 80, 81, 82,
    130
  political criticisms of, 50
  reform of, 56, 59
Local Government (NI) Act 1972, 72
Londonderry, 4, 7, 15, 31, 51, 53, 56,
    58
Lord Londonderry, 118
Lord Offaly, 14
Lundy, 17
Lyons, F. S. L., 24, 30, 118

MacDonagh, O., 21
Macrory Report, 59, 74ff.
manufacturing idustry, 9, 10
Marx, Karl, 153
Mason, Roy, 88, 142
Matthew Report, 72
McAllister, I., 54, 108, 112
McBride principles 85–6
McCrudden, C., 86
McCullagh and O'Dowd, 5, 8
McCuster, Harold, 144
Methodist Church, 8
Ministers (Northern Ireland) Act
    1921, 32
Ministry of Community Relations, 90
Ministry of Defence, 121
Ministry of Health and Local
    Government, 90
Ministry of Home Affairs, 90
Moloney, E. and Pollock, A., 101,
    103, 104, 105
Monaghan, 4
Moody, T. W., 23
Morrison, Danny, 111
Mullen, K., 86
Murie, A., 9, 31, 46, 90, 98, 102,
    127, 131

Nationalism, 23, 98
  nature of, 109ff.
Nationalist Party, 111–12
Nationalists, 30, 47, 52, 53, 57, 62,
    65, 68, 69, 94, 98, 102, 139,
    156, 157, 162, 163

attitude to Northern Ireland, 42
nature of, 109ff.
relationships with police, 43
Nelson, S., 103
New-Ireland Forum, 113–14, 145–6
  Report, 146–7
New University of Ulster, 52
NIC-ICTU, 119–20
Normans, 13
Northern Ireland Civil Rights
    Association, 50, 54, 55
Northern Ireland Civil Service
    (NICS), 32, 90ff., 117, 134–5
Northern Ireland Committee of the
    House of Commons, 95
Northern Ireland Constitutional Act
    1973, 87
Northern Ireland departments, 90,
    92, 93, 121, 124, 125
Northern Ireland Economic Council,
    9, 10, 123
Northern Ireland Hospitals
    Authority, 72
Northern Ireland Housing Executive
    (NIHE), 59, 80ff., 128ff.
  relationship with councils, 82, 130
  relationship with DOENI, 81–2,
    129ff.
Northern Ireland Housing Trust, 72
Northern Ireland MPs, 94
Northern Ireland Office, 83, 89, 94,
    121

O'Connell, Daniel, 21–2
O'Corrain, D., 13
O'Farrell, F., 21
O'Halloran, C., 156
O'Leary, C., 96, 143, 144
O'Malley, P., 103
O'Neill, Hugh, 14–15
O'Neill, Terence, 45, 47ff., 52, 55,
    56, 57, 104, 108, 119
Official Unionist Party (OUP), 64,
    65, 67, 80, 82, 101, 102, 103,
    104–5, 106, 107, 118, 139
Oliver, I., 83
Oliver, J., 59
Orange Order, 20, 25, 39, 40, 105,
    117–18, 152
Orders in council, 95, 143
Osbourne, R. D., 52, 86, 126

Paisley, Dr Ian, 48, 57, 65, 103, 104,
   105, 152
Pale, the, 13
parity, 36, 46, 91, 122
Parliament, 35, 48, 94ff.
Parnell, Charles, 24
partition, 26–7
Patten, J., 93
Pearse, 27
Peel, Robert, 22
penal laws, 18
People's Democracy, 56
Phoenix, E., 48
planning, 46, 52, 54, 73
plantations, 15ff.
police, 150
   Hunt Report, 83
   police deaths, 1, 68
   Royal Ulster Constabulary, 2, 4,
      43, 55, 58, 66, 83, 139, 150
Police Authority, 83ff.
policy communities, 116, 121ff.
Policy Co-ordinating Committee, 93
policy implementation, 133ff.
policy networks, 116, 122, 127,
   130–1, 136
policy-making, 115ff.
political divide, 98ff.
Pollock, 37
Poole, M. A., 128
Portadown, 39
poverty, 10, 154
power-sharing, 62, 64, 65, 109, 137,
   161–2
Power-Sharing Executive, 55, 62, 64,
   65, 113, 140–1
Presbyterian Church, 8, 26
Prior, James, 69, 132, 142, 144, 146
privatisation, 133
proportional representation, 35, 76
Protestants, 8, 15, 16, 17, 18, 19, 25,
   40, 41, 42, 51, 52, 53, 62, 68,
   98, 118, 126, 141, 152, 154,
   156, 159, 161
   as Irish Nationalists, 19–21, 25
Public Accounts Committee, 96
public expenditure, 9, 99, 122ff., 138,
   154
public finance devolved
   arrangements, 32, 36–7, 46,
   91–2, 122
   under Direct Rule, 122ff.
public sector, 9

Rees, Merlyn, 64, 87
religion, 7–8, 14–18, 118, 152ff.
Repeal of the Union, 22
Republic of Ireland, 39, 65, 68, 69,
   144, 145, 152, 155, 159
Rhodes, R., 116, 129
roads, 73
Robinson, Peter, 104, 106
rolling devolution, 69
Roman Catholics/Catholics, 7, 16,
   17, 18, 21, 22, 42, 48, 51, 52,
   53, 54, 59, 68, 84, 98, 102,
   103, 109, 118, 119, 126, 152ff.,
   154, 155, 156, 159
   attitude to IRA, 47, 67
   Catholic attitude to Northern
      Ireland, 35, 40–1, 42, 43, 48,
      109, 152
   Catholic Church and Irish
      Constitution, 37–8
   role in Free State, 37
Rose, R., 52, 98, 101, 109, 115, 161
Rowthorn, B. and Wayne, N., 9, 153
Royal Irish Constabulary, 42

Sands, Bobby, 67
Sarsfield, 17
Saunders, P., 117
Scotland, 4, 12, 15, 116, 123, 125
Secretary of State, 69, 87ff., 121,
   124, 125, 132, 148, 157
sectarian violence in Northern
   Ireland, 39
shipbuilding, 10, 23
Simms, K., 13
Sinclair, K., 77
Singleton, D., 55, 80, 128, 129
Sinn Fein, 28, 33, 67, 77, 78, 101,
   106, 109, 110ff., 150, 156
Smyth, C., 104
Social Democratic and Labour Party,
   61, 62, 67, 69, 78, 80, 101,
   110, 112ff., 139, 140, 143, 144,
   145, 156
social security, 124
Special Constabulary, 43, 50, 58, 59,
   83
Special Powers Act, 43, 50
Stalker, John, 150
Stewart, A. T. Q., 40, 147
Stormont, 31ff., 54, 62, 65, 91, 127
'Strongbow', 13

structure of Central Government, 90ff.
Sunningdale, 64

textiles, 10
Thatcher, Margaret, 69, 131, 133, 144, 147
'the Pale', 13
Todd, J., 101, 102
Townshend, C., 3, 27
trade unions, 119–20
Treasury, 91, 92, 122, 123, 124, 125
Treaty, 1921, 28, 32–4, 38
Treaty of Limerick, 17
Tyrone, 4, 7, 15, 31, 34

Ulster, 13ff., 23, 26, 27
Plantations, 15ff.
Ulster Defence Association (UDA), 64, 101, 103, 107–8, 140
Ulster Defence Regiment, 1, 59, 68, 83
Ulster Volunteer Force (UVF), 26, 27, 43, 49, 101, 108
Ulster Workers' Council (UWC), 64–5, 140–2
Ulster Workers' Council Strike, 65, 107, 140–2
unemployment, 9–10
Union, 21ff.
Unionism
nature of, 101ff.
Unionists, 20, 30, 33, 34, 42, 47, 48, 52, 53, 54, 56, 57, 61, 62, 69, 82, 94, 98, 105, 111, 118, 120, 139, 141, 142, 143, 146, 151, 157, 158, 159, 162, 163
Agreement, 69–70, 77, 106–7, 149–51

attitude to Catholics, 40–1, 102–3
attitude to rest of Ireland, 38
United Irishmen, 19–21
United Kingdom, 4, 6, 9, 10
United Ulster Unionist Council, 64, 65

Vanguard Party, 65
violence, 1, 2, 11, 39–40, 56, 57, 60, 61, 64, 67, 82, 103, 113, 142
deaths due to, 1, 2, 99

Wales, 4, 10, 116, 123
Wallace, M., 51
water, 73
Welfare State, 46, 48
West Belfast, 155
West, Harry, 67
Westminster, 31, 54, 55, 71, 91, 92, 94–6, 97, 111, 127
relations with Stormont, 31, 35, 46, 61, 91
Wexford, 16
Wheatley Report, 73
White, B., 48, 86
Whitehall, 91, 92, 93, 97, 117, 125, 126, 132
Whitelaw, William, 62
Whyte, John, 37, 38, 54, 151
William of Orange, 17
Wilson, Harold, 55, 65
Wilson, Sammy, 104
Wolfe Tone, 19–21
Woodham-Smith, C., 22
Workers' Party, 9, 110–11, 112, 154
Wright, F., 101, 102

Young, Arthur, 60